Religious Liberty and Education

Religious Liberty and Education

A Case Study of Yeshivas vs. New York

Edited by Jason Bedrick, Jay P. Greene, and
Matthew H. Lee

ROWMAN & LITTLEFIELD
Lanham • Boulder • New York • London

Published by Rowman & Littlefield
An imprint of The Rowman & Littlefield Publishing Group, Inc.
4501 Forbes Boulevard, Suite 200, Lanham, Maryland 20706
www.rowman.com

6 Tinworth Street, London SE11 5AL, United Kingdom

British Library Cataloguing in Publication Information Available

Library of Congress Cataloging-in-Publication Data

Names: Bedrick, Jason, editor. | Greene, Jay P., 1966- editor. | Lee,
    Matthew H., 1989- editor.
Title: Religious liberty and education : a case study of yeshivas vs. New
    York / edited by Jason Bedrick, Jay P. Greene, and Matthew H. Lee.
Description: Lanham, Maryland : Rowman & Littlefield Publishers, 2020. |
    Includes bibliographical references and index. | Summary: "Uses an
    ongoing legal controversy to explore the controversial subject of
    religious liberty and education"-- Provided by publisher.
Identifiers: LCCN 2020007477 (print) | LCCN 2020007478 (ebook) | ISBN
    9781475854398 (cloth) | ISBN 9781475854404 (paperback) | ISBN
    9781475854411 (epub)
Subjects: LCSH: Education--Curricula--Law and legislation--New York (State)
    | University of the State of New York--Trials, litigation, etc. | Jewish
    day schools--Law and legislation--New York (State) | Ultra-Orthodox
    Jews--Education--Law and legislation--New York (State) | Church
    schools--Law and legislation--New York (State) | Religious
    minorities--Education--Law and legislation--New York (State)
Classification: LCC KFN5664 .R45 2020 (print) | LCC KFN5664 (ebook) | DDC
    344.747/077--dc23
LC record available at https://lccn.loc.gov/2020007477
LC ebook record available at https://lccn.loc.gov/2020007478

Contents

Preface

Who Should Decide What Constitutes an Acceptable Education, Parents or the State?

Teach a child the way he should go, and even when he is old, he will not depart from it.
—Proverbs 22:6

On November 20, 2018, New York state education commissioner MaryEllen Elia announced new "guidelines" regarding compliance with the state's requirement that all private schools provide an education that is "substantially equivalent" to that offered by the public schools.[1] Although written in general terms, the guidelines were widely understood to be directed primarily at certain Orthodox Jewish day schools, or "yeshivas,"[2] that critics alleged were failing to provide a basic level of secular education.[3]

The guidelines included more stringent standards for which subjects must be taught (11 in total) and how much time must be spent on them (17.5 hours weekly). The guidelines also established a regime of school inspections by state and local officials. A school determined to be noncompliant was in danger of losing access to public aid programs (e.g., textbooks, transportation, and lunches) or even of having the state direct parents to enroll their children elsewhere or have their children deemed truant.

The response was swift and fierce. Private schools—not only the targeted yeshivas, but also other Jewish schools as well as Catholic, Protestant, and secular independent schools—joined forces to oppose the guidelines in the court of public opinion and the court of law. Coalitions of the schools filed three separate lawsuits against the guidelines, and their supporters wrote op-eds and lobbied their elected officials.

The opposition to more onerous regulations by the non-Jewish schools caught yeshiva critics by surprise. The regulations were intended to target only the yeshivas, and their critics assumed the Catholic and elite private schools could "easily pass any state inspection," and therefore would not be troubled by the new guidelines.[4] What the yeshiva critics failed to understand was the broader context and implications of the new guidelines for private schooling generally.

The New York yeshiva controversy raises fundamental philosophical, policy, and legal questions with ramifications far beyond the yeshiva walls or even the borders of New York State. State constitutions empower state governments with the duty to provide resident children with an education. They also protect parents' freedom of conscience and free religious exercise.

The interplay between these rights and duties leaves many unanswered questions. Who bears the primary responsibility for ensuring that children receive a quality education, parents or the state? Who gets to decide what the minimum standard of an education should be? When the desires of parents conflict with the dictates of state policy makers, who should prevail and under what circumstances? Do parents have a religious liberty interest that constitutionally outweighs a state's interest in having citizens learn certain skills and content it considers necessary for an educated citizenry?

How these questions are answered by policy makers and the courts will, to varying degrees, affect all private education providers and the parents who seek out their services.

The differing philosophical, legal, and practical perspectives found in this volume as well as the long history of controversy over state efforts to regulate yeshiva and other types of religious education suggests that these issues are unlikely ever to be fully resolved.

The arrangements that societies adopt as interim solutions are more likely to be political solutions, responding to the power and organizational capacity of competing interests, rather than philosophical or legal resolutions flowing from the logical merits of competing arguments. That is, the nature and extent of state regulation of religious education is determined more by power than principle.

If that is the case, why devote an edited volume to debating the legal and philosophical principles of state regulation of New York's yeshivas?

Our effort is motivated by a faith, perhaps as deep as any found in traditional religions, that how we determine our principles today shapes the interests around which we organize and use power to pursue in the future. This volume is very unlikely to have any effect on how the current yeshiva controversy is resolved, but it may help lay the foundations for how future controversies over religious education are resolved many years from now by influencing what people are inclined to think is reasonable and in their interest.

The long-term nature of our project helps explain why we are doing this as a published book, rather than as a series of op-eds or magazine articles. Religious liberty in education is an enduring issue and we hope this volume focused on a current conflict might serve as an enduring resource.

NOTES

1. New York State Education Department, "NYSED Releases Updated Guidance and Resources on Substantial Equivalency of Instruction," November 20, 2018, http://www.nysed.gov/news/2018/nysed-releases-updated-guidance-and-resources-substantial-equivalency-instruction.

2. This book uses the Hebrew term "yeshiva," and its Anglicized plural form "yeshivas," to refer to Orthodox Jewish day schools where children spend a majority or the entirety of the day on religious study.

3. Katie Honan, "State Issues New Curriculum Guidelines in Wake of Yeshiva Probe," *Wall Street Journal*, November 20, 2018, https://www.wsj.com/articles/state-issues-new-curriculum-guidelines-in-wake-of-yeshiva-probe-1542759784.

4. Shlomo Noskow, "Elite Private Schools Help Keep Yeshivas in the Dark," *Crain's New York*, April 12, 2019, https://www.crainsnewyork.com/op-ed/elite-private-schools-help-keep-yeshivas-dark-ages.

Introduction

Yeshivas vs. New York

BACKGROUND: JEWS AND EDUCATION

The New York yeshiva controversy concerns a particular, and relatively small, segment of the American Jewish community. Jews constitute about 2 percent of the American population, of whom 10 percent identify as Orthodox.[1] The Orthodox community itself is remarkably diverse, but it is united in its fidelity to observing Jewish law and its heavy emphasis on religious study. *Talmud Torah keneged kulam*, declares the Mishnah, *the study of Torah is equivalent to all* [other religious obligations].[2]

Among Orthodox Jews, therefore, the near-universal norm is to enroll their children in yeshivas, at least through high school.[3] As of 2013, the last year in which a thorough count was conducted, yeshivas educated more than 151,000 students in New York State.[4] If the New York yeshivas were a school district, in 2019 they would rank in the top 20 largest nationally, just behind the Dallas Independent School District and ahead of Charlotte-Mecklenburg and Philadelphia.[5]

Different streams of Orthodoxy vary considerably in their approach to secular studies. At one end of the spectrum, "Modern Orthodox" Jews tend to embrace secular study. Graduates of Modern Orthodox yeshivas regularly go on to study at mainstream universities.

At the other end of the spectrum are groups that see secular education as a wasteful distraction from religious education or even as undesirable due to particular content. This includes some portions of the Haredi community,[6] though the majority of Haredi yeshivas provide secular education. Those who object strenuously enough to secular education requirements that they are willing to risk confrontation with government officials are the subject of the present controversy.

These differing approaches to education among traditional Jews go back thousands of years. As Ira Stoll explains at greater length at the end of this volume, the Talmud records that the majority of the rabbinic sages favored a rigorous religious education combined with instruction in a trade, while a minority opinion is preserved that favored an exclusive focus on Torah study.

At Haredi yeshivas today, girls tend to receive a more robust education in secular subjects than boys. Boys tend to have long school days, often beginning around 7:30 a.m. and finishing around 6:00 p.m. in middle school and sometimes after 9:30 p.m. in high school.[7] Generally speaking, the Haredi yeshivas teach math, English, social studies, and science (often in Yiddish) in the afternoon, although the central focus is on religious education. Nevertheless, many of the top-scoring schools on the New York State exam, the Regents, are Haredi yeshivas.[8]

Yeshiva students spend most of the day studying the canon of Jewish texts, primarily the Torah and Talmud along with the vast body of ancient and medieval commentaries on them. As Professor Moshe Krakowski of Yeshiva University explains:

> In-class activities focused on these texts more closely resemble upper-level humanities coursework in a university than clerical training or contemplation of the Divine.
>
> Enter a college course on any subject in the humanities, and you'll likely find students working to parse the flow and meaning of primary texts, grappling with questions like "Who wrote this?," "What were they trying to say?," "Who was this written for?," "What were they arguing against?"
>
> This is not so different from what yeshiva kids spend most of their time doing—except that unlike most American university students, yeshiva kids are reading ancient and late ancient texts in their original languages (Biblical Hebrew, Mishnaic Hebrew, and Aramaic) rather than in translation.[9]

Students often study in pairs ("chavrusas") to decipher, engage with, and argue over the text and its commentaries using logic and evidence. As Krakowski notes, this "academic endeavor revolves around argumentation skills such as reasoning from evidence, resolving multiple perspectives, and contextualization among many others"—skills that are highly useful in "nearly every secular domain."[10]

Most of all, yeshiva education (like all education) is intended to socialize students to become good members of their society. As Krakowski explains, the yeshivas' aim "is to produce students who will remain committed to religious observance and lifelong Torah study, but who will also be able to raise and support a family, engage in a productive secular occupation if they wish to do so, and contribute to society."[11] Everything the yeshivas do is intended to further these goals.

THE STRUGGLE FOR JEWISH EDUCATION

As a religious minority, Jews have long had to contend with outside attempts to regulate or even prohibit Jewish education. These struggles have been indelibly imprinted in Jewish memory, often via ritual.

For example, the festival of Hanukkah celebrates the victory of the Jews over the Seleucid Empire, which, under Antiochus IV, sought to ban the Jewish faith. The Yom Kippur liturgy evokes the "Ten Martyrs," rabbis slain by the Roman government—one of whom was burned alive while wrapped in a Torah scroll. On Tisha B'Av, in addition to commemorating the two times the Holy Temple in Jerusalem was destroyed—by the Babylonians in about 587 B.C.E. and by the Romans circa 70 C.E.—Jews also recall the repeated pogroms, expulsions, inquisitions, massacres, and persecution they suffered for their fidelity to the Torah.

Some of these memories are of very recent vintage. In the twentieth century, the Soviet Union outlawed Jewish education along with instruction of other religions. Jewish families were required to enroll their children in public schools in which they were indoctrinated against the faith of the families and forebears.

"The solution of the Jewish problem in Russia lies in the fusion of the Jews in the great melting pot of the peoples who inhabit the Soviet Union," declared Anatol Lunatcharsky, Soviet commissar of education, in 1928. "We won't permit the opening of schools in Hebrew, a dead language."[12] Whereas the Nazis' "solution" to the so-called Jewish problem was to eradicate Jewish lives, the Soviet Communists sought to eradicate the Jewish soul.

To survive, several Jewish groups—particularly the Chabad-Lubavitch Hasidim[13]—organized networks of underground yeshivas to clandestinely educate Jewish children.[14] By the late 1920s, one such network, the Committee of Rabbis, operated about three dozen Jewish schools with an enrollment of about five thousand students.[15] Those caught operating illicit yeshivas by the Soviet secret police—often with the assistance of the *Evsektsiia*, a special section made up of secularized Jews loyal to the Communist Party—were subject to arrest, imprisonment, years of hard labor in Siberia, torture, and even death.[16]

Even today, traditional Jews must sometimes contend with government authorities to educate their children. For example, in 2019, Sweden's Supreme Court ruled that an Orthodox Jewish family must pay more than $100,000 in fines and court costs for illegally homeschooling their two youngest children.[17] Since there were no Jewish schools in the area, Rabbi

Alexander and Leah Namdar homeschooled and provided private tutoring for the nine oldest of their eleven children, all of whom passed the national exams and are gainfully employed.[18] However, in 2011 they ran afoul of a new law banning homeschooling except for "special circumstances."

Unfortunately for them, the law did not consider religion or safety to be valid exceptions.

The United Kingdom, home of the world's sixth-largest Jewish population, is increasingly hostile to traditional Jewish schools. As described in greater detail in chapter 7, the British Office of Standards in Education (Ofsted) has recently begun issuing failing grades to a number of Orthodox schools based primarily on their religious views and practices. For example, the private Vishnitz Girls School was repeatedly failed despite Ofsted finding that their teachers had "good subject knowledge and high-quality classroom resources" and a school culture that "focused on teaching pupils to respect everybody, regardless of beliefs and lifestyle."

What they were lacking, according to Ofsted, was a "full understanding of British values."[19] By this, Ofsted was not referring to respect for the monarchy or the Beatles, but rather that the school did not teach children about "gender reassignment and sexual orientation"—even though, at the time, the school was only for children ages three to eight. After public outcry, Ofsted quietly revised their report, eliminating all references to sexual orientation and gender identity.[20]

The commitment of Americans to the U.S. Constitution's guarantee of religious liberty has made America a much more hospitable environment for Jewish education, but even here traditional Jews have sometimes encountered obstacles.

In the early days of the republic, some states funded Jewish schools alongside other religious schools.[21] However, the rise of the "common school" movement in the late nineteenth century, combined with nativist sentiment directed primarily at Catholic immigrants, led to the public defunding of "sectarian" schools. The public schools were originally de facto nondenominational Protestant, leading prayers and using a translation of the Bible amenable to most Protestant denominations, meaning that Catholics, Jews, and other non-Protestants essentially had to pay for education twice: once to educate the children of their Protestant neighbors via taxes and again for their own children via tuition.

Though the public schools were eventually secularized, Orthodox Jews and other religious minorities who value an immersive religious education are no better off. Nevertheless, historically Jews in America have been, by and large, free to operate their private schools as they saw fit.

One exception to that freedom came in 1939, when yeshivas in New York came under government scrutiny over what and how they were educating their students. The New York State Board of Regents adopted a resolution advising certain "private or parochial schools that operate with a program providing a session carried on in a foreign language during the forenoon, with only an afternoon session in English" that they were in violation of the compulsory education law.[22]

Although the resolution was not explicit, it was clear to all which schools were intended. As historian Marvin Schick explains, "All 26 yeshivas then in existence in New York had a dual curriculum, with Jewish studies beginning in the morning and continuing into early afternoon. In the state's eyes, they were all in violation of the law, and all were at risk of having their charters revoked. That would have meant the end of yeshiva education in New York."[23]

The board gave the yeshivas until September 1, 1939, to reorganize their schedules, but eventually consented to grant an additional year. The yeshivas, however, refused to budge. In March of 1942, the board expressed frustration that "a number of schools have not complied with this requirement, in spite of repeated urgings by the Education Department," and passed a resolution authorizing the department to notify noncompliant private schools that their charters were subject to revocation pending a subsequent hearing.[24]

In July of 1942, prominent members of the Jewish community testified at the board of regents hearing in support of the yeshivas, including a state senator who served as a board member of one of the yeshivas. Following the hearing, the board formed a committee composed of senior department officials and representatives of the yeshivas and suggested that the department conduct school visits. None of the yeshivas were closed down.

ORIGINS OF THE CONTEMPORARY NYC YESHIVA CONTROVERSY

The contemporary yeshiva controversy began in 2011 with the formation of Young Advocates for Fair Education (YAFFED). Its founder, Naftuli Moster, and several other YAFFED members attended Haredi schools growing up and later wished they had received a more robust secular education.

Moster, who graduated summa cum laude from the College of Staten Island and earned a master's degree in social work from Hunter College, lamented to the *New York Times* that he was in college when he first heard the word "molecule." When he realized he was the only one in class who didn't know what it meant, he "felt embarrassed and ashamed."[25] "Every single time I didn't know something," he told the *Times*, "I thought, 'I'm too crippled to make it through.'" Determined that no other child should have to endure a similar experience, Moster formed YAFFED.

YAFFED asserts that many yeshivas fail to provide instruction that is "substantially equivalent" to public schools, as required by state law, and that some even leave students without the "sound basic education" required by New York State's constitution.[26] Over the last decade, YAFFED has engaged in numerous public relations campaigns—op-eds, rallies, billboards, letter-writing drives, etc.—to pressure the yeshivas to include a more robust secular curriculum or, more frequently, to pressure city and state officials into forcing them to do so.

In December 2014, YAFFED began pressuring city officials to investigate whether yeshivas were in compliance with the law. In July 2015, after a few attempts that got little traction, YAFFED published a letter signed by 52 "yeshiva graduates, teachers, and parents" alleging that 39 yeshivas (out of 275 citywide) failed to teach an adequate level of secular instruction.[27] This time, they received a response from the New York City Department of Education (DOE), which agreed to investigate the named yeshivas. Following this announcement, though, the DOE was silent on the matter for some time.

In the meantime, YAFFED conducted its own probe. In September 2017, the group released an investigative report that, among other things, criticized the DOE for its silence.[28] It also recommended that the department establish a task force to improve education in yeshivas, in particular by demanding that certain schools increase the amount of time devoted to secular studies. They further insisted that the DOE and the New York State Education Department (NYSED) "discontinue all funding to yeshivas" that fail to comply with the new regulations. Despite this call to action, the DOE did not immediately pursue YAFFED's recommendations.[29]

The next year, supporters of the yeshivas in the state legislature attempted to protect them from the DOE's involvement via a controversial amendment to the state budget. State senator Simcha Felder, an important swing vote whose constituency includes a large number of Orthodox Jews, sponsored an amendment relaxing the substantial equivalency requirement for nonprofit institutions that offer bilingual instruction and long school days—parameters that apply to virtually all Orthodox Jewish day schools in New York, but few if any others.[30]

To this end, it granted discretion to the NYSED commissioner to determine whether those schools meet the substantial equivalency standard, and encouraged the consideration of whether such schools "provide academically rigorous instruction that develops critical thinking skills . . . the outcomes of which, taking into account the entirety of the curriculum, result in a sound basic education."[31] On April 12, New York Governor Andrew Cuomo signed the bill into law.

Things moved swiftly after that. On July 23, YAFFED filed a federal lawsuit against Governor Cuomo, Board of Regents Chancellor Betty Rosa, and NYSED Commissioner MaryEllen Elia. It claimed, among other things, that the "vague" language in the Felder amendment created an unjust carve-out for Haredi schools in violation of the U.S. Constitution's Establishment Clause by "impermissibly aid[ing] religion and entangl[ing] the government with religion."[32]

Describing the amendment as "the result of a deliberately timed plan to hijack the negotiations for a New York state budget," the lawsuit detailed YAFFED's efforts to press the DOE for information related to its investigation into the yeshivas. On August 15—less than a month after the YAFFED suit was filed but nearly three years after it had declared its intent to investigate the yeshivas—the DOE released the preliminary results of its investigation.

In a letter to NYSED Commissioner Elia, New York City Chancellor Richard Carranza explained that the department had thoroughly investigated fifteen of the thirty-nine schools named in the 2015 YAFFED complaint. It found that nine schools were "outside the scope of its inquiry" (because they had closed or were limited to postsecondary instruction) and reported to have had trouble arranging visits with the remaining fifteen.[33] Carranza requested guidance from NYSED on that and several other issues.

Carranza suggested that the DOE had received an overall positive impression of the educational practices of many of the fifteen yeshivas it had visited and conferred with, and that he was pleased with the steps schools were taking to improve their secular studies. He explained that the DOE had worked with Parents for Educational and Religious Liberty in Schools (PEARLS), a nonprofit organization that has developed curricula that are both acceptable to Haredi yeshiva leaders and in compliance with New York State regulations.

YAFFED commended the chancellor for his transparency but emphasized the necessity of investigating the remaining fifteen schools.

In January 2019, YAFFED's case was dismissed on the grounds that they lacked standing to sue, as the group had not demonstrated how it had been harmed by the Felder Amendment.[34]

Despite this loss in court, YAFFED's goals have been advanced through other means. For one thing, the Felder Amendment has been employed in ways its supporters likely didn't anticipate. As noted above, the NYSED used its newfound discretion over yeshivas to release extremely detailed guidelines for private schools in November 2018. It directed local school authorities (LSAs) to review the types of schools described by the amendment (primarily if not exclusively yeshivas) and to provide recommendations to the commissioner regarding their substantial equivalency.

These guidelines emphasized the commissioner's authority in this matter, as stipulated by the Felder Amendment. They also alluded to forthcoming "toolkits" that proved to be even more detailed. According to the guidelines, the commissioner could require parents or guardians to enroll their children in compliant schools within thirty to forty-five days (deemed a "reasonable timeframe") should their current school be found in violation of the substantial equivalency requirement or their children would be declared truant.

PRIVATE SCHOOLS FIGHT BACK

In March 2019, within four months of the NYSED guidelines' release, three entities filed lawsuits challenging them. The New York State Association of Independent Schools (NYSAIS) filed first, alleging that the rules were unconstitutional because neither NYSED nor the LSAs had specific, delegated authority from the legislature to investigate schools or to create their own standards for substantial equivalence. The association also argued that the guidelines violated the state Administrative Procedure Act (APA) because they constituted rules for the purposes of that statute and should therefore have gone through the administrative rulemaking process.

PEARLS, along with other yeshiva advocates, filed next. On March 7, they requested an injunction against the guidelines, along with a declaration that the guidelines were null and void on statutory, procedural, and constitutional grounds. In addition to NYSAIS's arguments, PEARLS argued that the guidelines violated the free-exercise rights of students and parents who wished to choose an education in line with their beliefs; the free-speech rights of the schools to teach as they wish; and the due-process rights of parents to direct their children's education.

In a third lawsuit filed on March 18, the New York State Council of Catholic School Superintendents reiterated several of the previous claims and also raised several additional arguments related to religious freedom.

On April 17, 2019, the New York State Supreme Court of Albany County, which is the trial-level court in the state, ruled that NYSED had not followed proper procedure when issuing the guidelines. Therefore, the guidelines were determined to be void. Having decided the case on statutory grounds, the court did not address the merits of the religious liberty claims.

In early July, the NYSED published a notice of proposed rulemaking in the state register, allowing for comments from the public until September 3.[35] In other words, they stated their intent to pass the same or similar regulations through the proper procedures. In the subsequent three months, until the public comment period closed, the department received more than 140,000 comments about the new guidelines, most of them in opposition.[36]

On December 19, 2019, NYSED released the results of its investigation. Out of twenty-eight yeshivas under investigation, the department determined that two met state guidelines, five lacked evidence of teaching English or math, twelve had secular education programs that were deemed insufficient, and the rest "didn't hit targets, but fared better and appeared to be making more of an effort to meet state expectations."[37]

ORGANIZATION OF THIS BOOK

To address the broader issues raised by the New York yeshiva controversy in this volume, some of the nation's leading thinkers examine the issue from a variety of perspectives. The book is organized into three main sections. In the first section, three authors seek to establish a theoretical foundation for determining when the state should interfere in the parent-child relationship to enforce the minimum requirements of an education.

In chapter 1, Kevin Vallier develops a three-pronged test for determining the conditions under which state intervention would be appropriate. He argues that it must be demonstrated that the educational interests of students are significantly threatened, that the intervention proposed by the state is not unnecessarily coercive, and that the government has demonstrated the ability to secure students' interests. Vallier discusses the extent to which he believes these conditions have been satisfied in the case of the yeshivas.

In chapter 2, Ashley Rogers Berner explores three frameworks for how much control the state, the individual, or civil society should have over education. Berner advocates for the pluralist framework, in which control over education rests primarily with civil society. In this framework, the state does not exclusively provide education but has an interest in enforcing basic standards of content.

In chapter 3, Rita Koganzon explains why the currently dominant liberal understanding of religious liberty and education may be insufficient. She argues that prominent liberal theorists, like John Rawls, Amy Gutmann, and Meira Levinson, posit that an important feature of education in a liberal society is that it promotes diversity and autonomy. Koganzon argues that the thriving communities, families, and individuals upon which liberal society depends may be undermined by an education that prioritizes autonomy above all else. The type of education found in yeshivas, she contends, actually tends to contribute to successful liberal societies.

The second section shifts from philosophy to law. In chapter 4, Aaron Saiger discusses how courts are likely to treat the constitutional claims of the yeshivas and what degree of regulation the state may constitutionally impose on private schools. According to Saiger, it is well established by the Supreme Court that reasonable regulation of the private school sector is constitutional, but that excessive or discriminatory regulation is unconstitutional. For the yeshivas and the State of New York, the relevant question to be answered is what degree and type of regulation of the yeshivas can be considered "reasonable."

Chapter 5 moves from the describing what the law *is* to what the law *should be*. Howard Slugh and Devorah Goldman argue for revisiting certain constitutional precedents in order to provide greater protections to religious families. Given the constitutional issues surrounding the yeshiva case, as well as the precedents established in landmark Supreme Court cases on religious liberty including *Smith* (1990), *Lukumi* (1993), and *Masterpiece Cakeshop* (2017), what options do—and should—the yeshivas have?

In chapter 6, Charles Glenn addresses how the tensions between parental control, religious freedom, and education have been resolved in various European contexts, which vary widely in how they address religious liberty and regulate education. Key differences in the legal tradition of the United States and these various European countries may limit the extent to which they inform the legal battle over the New York yeshivas. But the experience in Europe may suggest what U.S. religious education could expect depending on how U.S. authorities choose to resolve current conflicts.

In our final section, four authors consider the implications for various communities if a state were to vigorously enforce a "substantial equivalency" statute. Avi Schick opens in chapter 7 with the implications for the community most directly affected by the case: Haredi Jews. Schick fears that proposed regulations will diminish the study of the Torah, which is widely regarded by Orthodox Jews as one of the most central activities of Jewish life. Moreover, the power to restrict the teaching of certain subjects may effectively become the ability to dictate which values the yeshivas must teach their students.

The New York yeshiva controversy has implications for other communities as well. In chapter 8, Jay Ferguson discusses how Christian private schools may be affected. According to Ferguson, the mandate that private schools must provide a "substantially equivalent" education will compromise the principles that serve as the foundation for a substantially *dissimilar* Christian education.

Among these principles is the belief that truth is revealed by God to man, a concept shared in the Muslim education tradition, which Jibran Khan describes in chapter 9. Muslim education in madrasas bears many similarities to Jewish education in yeshivas, including the study of religious texts in their original languages. In many countries throughout the Muslim world, madrasas are strictly regulated by their respective governments. Khan discusses the implications of similar regulations for madrasas in the United States.

Although their children are educated in nonschool environments, the "substantial equivalence" requirement also has implications for homeschoolers. The diverse motivations for homeschooling bear an important similarity: the desire to choose an education that differs significantly from what is offered by traditional public schools. In chapter 10, Michael Donnelly discusses why "substantial equivalence" is an impractical and impermissible standard for regulating homeschooling.

The controversy surrounding the yeshivas centers on how to strike the right balance between the pursuit of a secular education and the study of sacred texts, such as the Torah and the Talmud. In chapter 11, Ira Stoll concludes the book by reflecting on two Talmudic passages in which rabbis debate this very issue to see what guidance Jewish texts have to offer for how this controversy should be resolved.

The contributors to this volume represent a diverse set of views on the yeshiva controversy in particular, and the role of religious liberty in education more generally. These issue tend to be deeply personal and provoke sometimes passionate disputes. We hope that this volume brings a more levelheaded approach that helps readers think more clearly about the roles of the state and parents in educating children.

NOTES

1. Ira Sheshkin and Arnold Dashefsky, "United States Jewish Population, 2018," *Current Jewish Population Reports* (New York: Berman Jewish DataBank, 2019), 18, https://www.jewishdatabank.org/content/upload/bjdb/2018-United_States_Jewish_Population_(AJYB,_Sheskin,_Dashefsky)_DB_Final.pdf; Pew Research Center, "A Portrait of American Orthodox Jews," *Religion and Public Life*, August 26, 2015, 2, https://www.pewforum.org/2015/08/26/a-portrait-of-american-orthodox-jews/. "The 2013 survey found that Orthodox Jews make up about 10% of the estimated 5.3 million Jewish adults (ages 18 and older) in the United States."

2. Mishnah Peah 1:1.

3. Pew Research Center, 2015, 11. Eighty-one percent of Orthodox parents of children of school age enroll those children in full-time, private Jewish schools.

4. Menachem Wecker, "New York State Cracks Down on Jewish Schools," *Education Next* 19, no. 40 (Fall 2019), https://www.educationnext.org/new-york-state-cracks-down-jewish-schools-senator-simcha-felder-rabbi-chaim-dovid-zwiebel-joseph-hodges-choate/.

5. Niche.com, "Largest School Districts in America," 2020 Best Schools, 2019, https://www.niche.com/k12/search/largest-school-districts/.

6. "Haredi" means "one who trembles," that is, trembles in the presence of God (cf. Isaiah 66:2, 5). The meaning is similar to the Quakers or Shakers, though they are theologically and sociologically quite different. Though the term "ultra-Orthodox" is more commonly found in the media, it carries a pejorative connotation and is rarely used as a self-description. Haredi Jews (*pl.* "Haredim") include Hasidic Jews and several non-Hasidic communities within Orthodoxy.

7. Moshe Krakowski, "What Yeshiva Kids Are Actually Studying All Day," *The Forward*, December 26, 2018, https://forward.com/life/faith/416616/what-yeshiva-kids-are-actually-studying-all-day/.

8. Moshe Krakowski, "The Truth about Secular Studies in Haredi Schools," *The Forward*, September 19, 2019, https://forward.com/opinion/431757/the-truth-about-secular-studies-in-haredi-schools/; Sandy Eller, "Regents Data: Public Schools Lag Behind Yeshivas," *The Jewish Press*, December 12, 2018, http://www.jewishpress.com/news/us-news/ny/regents-scores/2018/12/12/.

9. Krakowski, 2018.

10. Ibid.

11. Krakowski, 2019.

12. Jewish Telegraphic Agency, "Soviet Education Commissar Advises Jews to Fuse in Russian Melting Pot," archive, October 12, 1928, https://www.jta.org/1928/10/12/archive/soviet-education-commissar-advises-jews-to-fuse-in-russian-melting-pot.

13. Ibid. Lunatcharsky himself threatened, "We will combat the relics of the Middle Ages, the Schneersohnovschina," referring to the sixth Lubavitcher Rebbe, Rabbi Yosef Yitzchak Schneersohn, who was then directing underground activities from exile in Latvia after having been arrested—and nearly executed—by the Soviet secret police. See also Dovid Margolin, "The Roots of Today's Revival of Russian Judaism Lie Deep in the Soviet Past," *Mosaic Magazine*, March 23, 2017, https://mosaicmagazine.com/response/history-ideas/2017/03/the-roots-of-todays-revival-of-russian-judaism-lie-deep-in-the-soviet-past/.

14. Zvi Y. Gitelman, *Jewish Nationality and Soviet Politics* (Princeton: Princeton University Press, 2015), Project MUSE, http://muse.jhu.edu/book/38639.

15. David E. Fishman, "Committee of Rabbis in the USSR," YIVO Encyclopedia of Jews in Eastern Europe, August 2, 2010, https://yivoencyclopedia.org/article.aspx/Committee_of_Rabbis_in_the_USSR.

16. Ibid. See also Jewish Telegraphic Agency, "Leaders of Minsk Kehillah Arrested by G.P.U.; Charged with Counter-Revolution," archive, February 17, 1930, https://www.jta.org/1930/02/17/archive/leaders-of-minsk-kehillah-arrested-by-g-p-u-charged-with-counter-revolution.

17. Cnaan Liphshiz, "Chabad Couple Made to Pay $100K for Homeschooling Their Children in Sweden," *The Jerusalem Post*, June 22, 2019, https://www.jpost.com/Diaspora/Chabad-couple-made-to-pay-100K-for-homeschooling-their-children-in-Sweden-593287.

18. The Yeshiva World, "Sweden: $67,000 Fine for Homeschooling of Children of Chabad Shluchim," *The Yeshiva World*, June 13, 2019, https://www.theyeshivaworld.com/news/israel-news/1741840/sweden-67000-fine-for-homeschooling-of-children-of-chabad-shluchim.html.

19. Jibran Khan, "Amanda Spielman's War on Religion in Great Britain," *National Review Online*, January 28, 2019, https://www.nationalreview.com/2019/01/amanda-spielman-religious-schools-england-secularism/.

20. Joe Kelly, "Backflip on School Gender Report," *The Australian*, November 3, 2017, https://www.theaustralian.com.au/nation/politics/vishnitz-backflip-by-uk-school-watchdog/news-story/aaeb68a8154fcc0e877a4a68cd3351d0.

21. Charles L. Glenn, *The Myth of the Common School* (Amherst: University of Massachusetts Press, 1988).

22. Marvin Schick, "As New York Once Again Targets Religious Schools, a History Lesson in Communal Resistance," *Tablet*, August 12, 2019, https://www.tabletmag.com/jewish-news-and-politics/289450/new-york-targets-religious-schools.

23. Ibid.

24. Ibid.

25. Jennifer Miller, "Yiddish Isn't Enough," *New York Times*, November 21, 2014, https://www.nytimes.com/2014/11/23/nyregion/a-yeshiva-graduate-fights-for-secular-studies-in-hasidic-education.html.

26. Young Advocates for Fair Education, "Press Release: Felder Amendment Lawsuit," July 23, 2018, https://www.yaffed.org/lawsuit1.

27. Amy Sara Clark, "Reversing Course, DOE Vows to Broaden Yeshiva Probe," *The New York Jewish Week*, October 8, 2015, https://jewishweek.timesofisrael.com/reversing-course-doe-vows-to-broaden-yeshiva-probe/.

28. Marci A. Hamilton and Louis Grumet, "Non-Equivalent: The State of Education in New York City's Hasidic Yeshivas," report (New York: Young Advocates for Fair Education, September 2017), https://www.yaffed.org/report.

29. Ibid., 10.

30. Amy Sara Clark, "Questions Over Felder's 'Yeshiva' Amendment," *The New York Jewish Week*, April 3, 2018, https://jewishweek.timesofisrael.com/questions-over-felders-yeshiva-amendment/.

31. New York State Assembly, Bill No. S07509, January 18, 2018, 194, https://nyassembly.gov/leg/?leg_video=&bn=S07509&term=2017&Floor%2526nbspVotes=Y&Text=Y.

32. Young Advocates for Fair Education v. Andrew Cuomo, 359 F. Supp. 3d 215 (E.D.N.Y. 2019), 32.

33. Richard Carranza, "Substantial Equivalence Inquiry," 2018; Steve Lipman, "Yeshiva Probe Report Seen Inconclusive," *The New York Jewish Week*, August 21, 2018, https://jewishweek.timesofisrael.com/yeshiva-probe-report-seen-inconclusive/.

34. Karen Matthews, "Lawsuit Over Amendment Shielding Some Jewish Schools Tossed," *Associated Press*, January 17, 2019, https://www.apnews.com/ab85f6b2aabc46498d0a6c94266bb1a6.

35. New York State Education Department, "State Education Department Proposes Regulations for Substantially Equivalent Instruction for Nonpublic School Students," May 31, 2019, http://www.nysed.gov/news/2019/state-education-department-proposes-regulations-substantially-equivalent-instruction.

36. Selim Algar, "State Hit with 140K Public Comments on Bid to Boost Private School Oversight," *New York Post*, September 11, 2019, https://nypost.com/2019/09/11/state-hit-with-140k-public-comments-on-bid-to-boost-private-school-oversight/.

37. Leslie Brody, "Investigators Say 26 Yeshivas Fall Below New York's Education Standards," *Wall Street Journal*, December 19, 2019, https://www.wsj.com/articles/investigators-say-26-yeshivas-fall-below-new-yorks-education-standards-11576798974/.

Part One

Philosophical Perspectives on Religious Liberty in Education

Chapter One

In Defense of Yeshiva Autonomy

Kevin Vallier

In recent years, progressive attitudes toward religious liberty have shifted dramatically, from the celebration that led to the 1993 Religious Freedom Restoration Act (RFRA), to forbearance and suspicion in the late 2010s. The shift from approval to hostility is due to changes in health-care and discrimination law, in particular opposition to religious exemptions from providing abortifacients and for wedding vendors who decline to serve same-sex weddings.

The earlier liberal consensus deserves defense. The growing hostility toward religious liberty, especially in health care and education, harms religious individuals and religious organizations. One example is attempts by New York State's education department to subject Hasidic yeshivas (Jewish primary schools) to considerable curriculum scrutiny. If these yeshivas do not meet vague yet nonetheless demanding curricular standards, New York State has threatened to shut the schools down and treat students who continue to attend these schools as truant, legally penalizing Jewish parents.

These hostile actions are prompted by former yeshiva students known as YAFFED (Young Advocates for Fair Education) who believe they were not given proper secular education needed to navigate their social world when they decided to leave their communities.[1]

Yeshiva autonomy should not be subject to the interventions proposed by YAFFED and the expected implementation of some of these interventions by New York State (NYS) and New York City (NYC). To demonstrate, this essay formulates a three-pronged test for when state intervention into childhood education is appropriate, and then argues that the proposed interventions do not satisfy the test. It argues that states may intervene into private religious school education under three conditions:

1. when the educational interests of children are significantly threatened,
2. when the intervention is the least coercive effective means to protect educational interests, and
3. when the government has demonstrated its ability to secure the educational interests of children better than the religious schools themselves.

These conditions are not satisfied in the case of New York's yeshivas. First, it appears that the educational interests of children are adequately protected, or at least that the evidence that their interests have been harmed is meager at best. Second, the proposed remedies are disproportionate to the harms documented. And finally, it is not clear that NYS and NYC have the ability to improve educational outcomes in these schools.

Given some plausible conditions that regulate the moral justification of state coercion, and an adequate conception of the educating and educational interests of religious communities and students, the newly proposed restrictions on yeshivas cannot be justified.

STATE COERCION, RELIGION, AND EDUCATION

A fundamental principle of any free society is a *presumption against state coercion*.[2] The state has no automatic license to coercively interfere with its citizens. Rather, coercion must be justified; otherwise, people should be free to order their own lives. This essay takes the presumption for granted, as well as its application to individuals, the family, schools, and houses of worship.

What considerations meet the presumption against coercion? Protecting the interests of children is an obvious one, including nutrition, health, shelter, clothing, education, familial relationships, protection from abuse and harm, etc. In the context of schooling, the prime interest at stake is the educational interests of children.

Education is a basic interest primarily for instrumental reasons: education facilitates acquiring other goods, such as employment, and more broadly, mastering skills and information that create meaningful lives. Education also has intrinsic value; some knowledge is worth having for its own sake.

People disagree about educational interests regarding religious instruction. Religious parents see religious education as central interests of children, since religion not only shapes a child's beliefs and character, but helps the child find meaning and perhaps to create an enduring relationship with God.

In contrast, secular parents typically see little value in religious instruction. In some cases, secular parents even argue that religious instruction frustrates the interests of children by instilling false and pernicious beliefs. But in the United States, secular parents are generally prepared to defer to religious parents in determining how to educate their children. This is because both religious and secular parents generally agree that parents should be able to make educational decisions for their children.

Other considerations that can meet the presumption against coercion are the interests of parents, families, and communities. Regarding religious matters, parents and communities have fundamental interests in *educating.* One point of agreement between many religious and secular citizens is that parents and communities have considerable autonomy in transmitting their values and beliefs to the next generation.[3] This educating interest is also the lifeblood of any association that hopes to ensure far into the future. Indeed, it is among the chief interests of "chinuch"—the Hebrew term for education and training, and one of the keys to Jewish continuity.

State coercion can be utilized in order to protect the *educational* interests of children and the *educating* interests of parents and communities, such as protecting private schools and administering public schools. But if the state is a danger to these interests, or it cannot secure these interests better than parents and communities themselves, the presumption against coercion is not met and state coercion is impermissible. For if state intervention harms educational and educating interests, it should abide by sharp restrictions on its power.

Given the presumption against coercion, states must also take the least coercive actions available to secure educational and educating interests. If government provision of education is the only way to secure the educational interests of children, then government provision may be justified.

But if government can protect the educational interests of children through enforcing standards on religious schools, then it must respect their autonomy. On a smaller scale, if governments can convince private schools to improve educational quality with modest fines rather than threatening parents of these children with jail time, then it must use these less restrictive means.

Third, the presumption against coercion implies that, in cases where states and communities, parents, and children *disagree* about what educational interests mean and how to interpret them, then the state should defer to the liberty of older children, parents, and communities about how those interests are to be understood. Though private education should adequately educate children in subjects that both parties agree are essential for a functional and flourishing childhood and adulthood.[4]

While my use of the presumption against coercion may strike some as excessively restrictive, note that this is not a prohibition on state coercion. The presumption concerns where the burden of proof lies and how the burden can be met. If the presumption is hard to meet, that is appropriate for any society that understands itself as liberal.

Now, let's turn to the content of educational and educating interests. What sorts of things should the state ensure that children are taught? At a minimum, children are owed education in basic skills for developing further skills, and navigating their physical and social world. Children are entitled to education in reading, writing, and mathematics, as well as some basic history, science, and health. Children are also owed an education in their basic freedoms, such as freedom of speech, press, and religion. In particular, children have the right to know that they are legally protected if they exit their communities.

One important question is whether the educational interests of children are set back if they do not have language skills in the dominant language of their culture, such as yeshiva students who have a rich understanding of Yiddish and Hebrew,[5] but who know very little English.

My sense is that children are certainly owed competence in at least one language, and have language skills that can be used to acquire competence in another language. So if yeshiva students are highly proficient in Yiddish and Hebrew, and have the ability to acquire English competence if they wish as they grow older, that need not seriously harm their educational interests. It is common in immigrant communities for students to only have skills in the languages they speak at home, and that is usually not taken as grounds for forcing children to learn English.

That said, children in a society that overwhelmingly speaks English have an educational interest in English competence. The question is whether these educational interests are strong enough to override the educating interests of their parents and community. As long as the children are highly competent in at least one language, that may often be sufficient to allow parents to decide which language they are raised within, so long as the linguistic community is not extremely small.[6]

But the political groups that are pushing for government oversight in these cases seldom raise concerns that, say, members of minority linguistic communities like Hispanics must have full English competence. In a multicultural society, we may simply have many, distinct linguistic communities. Even so, basic English competence is in the interest of students, and so if yeshivas do not provide English competence, that is at least prima facie grounds for government to interfere.

One might worry more if students know very little math, since innumeracy can greatly hamper a person's ability to get a range of more challenging and high-paying jobs. So some math skills are necessary for the educational interests of children, and for them to have an effective freedom of exit from their community.

While students have educational interests in a high school education, the reader need not worry too much if they lack competence in high school history and science, which they should be able to pick up in their own language when the information is necessary. Much of the information learned is not useful to people in the future, and little of it is required for students to have freedom of exit and effective freedom of occupation. Few jobs require competence in these areas.[7]

How, then, should the state balance the educational interests of children and the educating interests of parents and communities in cases where the educating interests of parents and communities are being used to block or undermine the educational interests of children?

First, the state must recognize a presumption in favor of leaving instruction in vital subjects to parents and communities, and allow them to choose their own way of conveying the relevant information.

Second, there is a presumption in favor of allowing parents and communities to provide extensive instruction in other important areas, such as religious instruction. States should only intervene, then, when religious community schools fail to convey nonreligious subject matters adequately, and should not intervene in the religious instruction of children at all if religious instruction does not conflict with conveying information essential to nonreligious subjects.

But if parents and communities are not providing students with basic English-language competence and mathematics, and they refuse to do so when asked and prompted, then that the state can deem that the educational interests of children override the educating interests of parents and communities.

YESHIVAS

We now have the moral and political principles necessary to address the yeshiva controversy, so let's review the facts of the case.

In Brooklyn, Orthodox Jewish schools have long been responsible for the religious education of children in those communities. Most religious education, but far from all, is reserved for males, who receive a large amount of religious instruction, considerably more not only than the general population, but than almost any other form of religious instruction in the United States.[8] The large majority of the school day for ultra-Orthodox/Haredi Jewish males is spent on a range of religious subjects, from studying the Hebrew Bible and Talmud directly, to commentaries and religious legal codes accumulated over thousands of years.

Nonetheless, Haredi Jews are trained in English, math, social studies, and science. And all religious instruction involves the extensive use of reading and writing, and often basic mathematics.[9] The rigor and depth of their religious education is stunning. Many children are learning legal concepts typically taught to young adults twice their age. They have much longer school days. And the amount of education they receive in many subjects is staggering.

Periodically, children educated in Haredi yeshivas leave the community, often joining more theologically liberal Jewish communities. A few have felt that they were unprepared for life outside of those communities, and formed YAFFED, which recently sued New York State, "challenging the constitutionality of a recent amendment to an education law directed at these schools," and arguing that their education in these schools is not "substantially equivalent" to that in public schools.[10] YAFFED opposed the amendment because, in their view, it let yeshivas off the hook in protecting the educational interests of children.

YAFFED lost the lawsuit due to lack of standing, so they pushed the NYS education department to formulate new guidelines. NYS has now released complex guidelines for what "substantial equivalence" means, which many yeshiva educators regard as grave challenges to the structure of their curriculum.[11] If the schools do not follow the relevant guidelines, New York State has threatened to shut down schools that do not meet them, and treat students who attend these schools as truant.

This is a considerable threat. It involves gravely coercive restrictions on the educating interests of parents and communities. If indeed such coercion is required to meet the educational interests of children, especially male children, in these schools, then perhaps it can be justified.

But if we bear the presumption against coercion in mind, we must view these actions as prima facie suspect, in particular because less coercive methods of protecting the interests of children are available, such as modest fines. Admittedly, given that Haredi parents remember running underground yeshivas in the Soviet Union, they may simply pay the fines and continue as before, but intermediate steps should still be taken.

The major controversy is how to determine when the substantial equivalency guidelines are met. The new law states that "the state education commissioner, rather than local school districts, will determine equivalency for schools that meet certain criteria that were drawn only to include Hasidic Yeshivas."[12] The Department of Education has even threatened to issue "lesson plans" to these schools.

In April of 2019, a state judge in Albany nullified these state educational guidelines on statutory grounds.[13] Judge Christina Ryba ruled that the new guidelines "were not implemented in compliance with the State Administrative Procedure Act" though she did not address whether the guidelines violated New York's constitutional protections for religious freedom. So for now, the guidelines are not in effect, but only on a legal technicality, and not on principled grounds. This means that it is possible that reformulated guidelines will be applied to yeshivas in the future.

YESHIVA AUTONOMY DEFENDED

To defend yeshiva autonomy, we must assess whether NYS and YAFFED's proposals meet our tripartite test. Are they necessary to protect the educational interests of children? Do the remedies use the least coercive means necessary to protect those interests? And are the remedies provided bearing in mind the limitations that New York State has in educating students in its own schools?

Let's begin with the first prong of the test—are educational interests harmed in these schools? YAFFED cites two sources of evidence that indeed this is the case. YAFFED first cites evidence from the yeshivas that administer some or all of the state tests on basic subjects like English Language Arts and mathematics. They state:

> Of those that have administered some or all of the tests, a very low percentage of students meet or exceed state standards. For example, on nearly all of this year's English Language Arts (ELA) and mathematics exams Bobover Yeshiva Bnei Zion has zero students achieving levels three or four, which are considered passing. More than 94% of the students who took any given test at the school received a level one score. Yeshiva Beth Hillel of Krasna and Yeshiva Machzikei Hadas saw similar results, with almost no students achieving levels three or four on any state examination. [14]

This information is public and is worrisome regarding ELA, and especially with regard to mathematics.

Second, YAFFED cites anonymous surveys that they have used to determine what is taught in 39 yeshivas it cites as at risk. The surveys have had about 116 respondents, though with anonymous surveys, it is not clear who the respondents are, whether they have sufficient acquaintance with these institutions, whether anyone answered more than once, and whether they are being truthful.

One problem is the number of respondents per school is low. One hundred sixteen graduates for 39 schools comes to 2.9 students per yeshiva, *assuming the students are evenly distributed between schools.* That's a low number already, and it is probably spread out over many years of education, and so many focus primarily on students who graduated anywhere from a few years ago to a decade or more. What's worse, the survey was only carried out through Facebook friends of members of YAFFED or its director, which suggests an extreme selection bias.

Further, when YAFFED filed a complaint, it had only 52 signatories. And when NYS interviewed them, only 11 were determined to have any connection with any of the schools noted. These interviews also led to the reduction of the number of schools on the at-risk list from 39 to 30. [15]

So the evidence that yeshivas are failing their students comes from the curriculum of at most 30 of 440 yeshivas in New York State from the testimony of only 11 of whom the state of New York could determine were somehow connected with these institutions. And this is in the face of contradictory testimony filed as affidavits from graduates of these schools.[16]

Now let us turn to what YAFFED proposes as remedies for their complaints:[17]

1. Yeshivas should begin to annually increase the amount of time spent on secular studies per day by at least 30 to 45 minutes.
2. Yeshivas should teach all state-mandated subjects for each grade level.
3. Yeshivas should spend a minimum of 3 hours on secular studies in elementary schools and 2.5 hours in high schools.
4. Yeshivas should administer Regents exams and provide diplomas to all high school graduates.[18]

These are big changes backed with big penalties. Worrisomely, YAFFED's report does not explain how they came up with these recommendations, and so they do not explain why these changes are not overly demanding to meet the educational interests of children. This lack of explanation leaves me with several concerns.

First, it is unclear that yeshiva education needs to be changed *at all*, just that students acquire the needed information and skills *in some way or another*, perhaps at home, with private tutors and computer-based learning. The educational interests of children do not require that their *main school* convey information or skills. YAFFED would need to show that independent educational efforts are unlikely to succeed.

Second, spending a minimum of 3 hours on secular studies comes with what the community regards as grave opportunity costs, because the more time spent on secular studies, the less time spent on religious studies, sometimes called "bitul Torah" or the nullification of the Torah implied by spending too much time on other subjects or activities.[19] The educating interests of parents and communities will be considerably set back by these requirements, especially if students can acquire the relevant information and skills with less time or effort.

Third, YAFFED's demand that yeshivas teach *all state-mandated subjects for every grade level* is surely a violation of the educating interests of parents and communities, and unnecessary to satisfy the basic educational interests of children. The additional information is unnecessary for effective freedom of exit and freedom of occupation. And these requirements would greatly hamper the educating interests of parents.

Finally, there are reasonable concerns about requiring all yeshivas to mandate state-created exams and to accept the regulations required by offering diplomas, since this allows NYS to increasingly control yeshiva curriculum by altering the tests.[20] It creates an incentive to teach to the test that parents and the community may reasonably object to.

So we have limited information about whether the educational interests of these children have been harmed, and the proposed remedies seem inappropriate and excessive.

Moreover, many of the schools claim that they have undertaken their own reforms. A pro-yeshiva advocacy group, PEARLS (Parents for Educational and Religious Liberty in Schools) has produced updated, culturally sensitive curricula for the students.[21]

Fortunately, NYS has yet to apply any penalties directly, but if they deem internal reform efforts unsuccessful, a reasonable intervention might begin with a request that all yeshivas select a method of determining the basic language competence and mathematical ability of their students. This would provide the state and the public with more information and would not be very burdensome on yeshivas, since they could choose the tests and choose when to hold them.

For yeshivas that refuse, NYS might apply a modest fine or withdraw certain public benefits that go directly to the schools. With further noncompliance, fines could be gradually increased, where necessary. NYS might also offer parents the opportunity to have their students tested at a community facility if schools refuse to run the tests. So long as the state has good information about linguistic and mathematical competence, that is enough to discharge its duties.

But we must consider the third prong of the test—are NYS and NYC competent to improve educational quality at these private schools? After all, there are many problems with NYS schools, and it is unclear that the imposition of testing and requirements in government schools have been sufficient to satisfy and protect the educational interests of children in their schools.

Consequently, it is not clear how much state intervention is likely to improve conditions in these yeshivas. But given the lower test scores of yeshiva students[22] who have been tested, NYS may be able to improve educational quality in at least mathematical ability, and if English is an educational interest, to improve English ability. So it is not clear whether the proposed intervention satisfies the third prong of our test for permissible state intervention—it might or might not.

Thus, yeshivas are not uniquely problematic in terms of meeting state standards. It appears that New York state schools do not do much better, and that's with students who have English as a first language and that spend far more time during the day on those subjects.[23]

I conclude, then, that NYS has not met the presumption against state coercion. It is unclear whether the educational interests of yeshiva students have been harmed, it is clear that the proposed penalties are excessive, and it's not obvious that NYS can improve educational quality given its own limited success in educating students in its own schools.

PUBLIC ASSISTANCE AND SUBSTANTIAL EQUIVALENCE — TWO YAFFED CRITICISMS ANSWERED

Before concluding, let's address two of YAFFED's arguments for their restrictions, both of which may strike the public as plausible, but that are problematic.

The first argument is that New York State law requires that students be guaranteed an education that is "substantially equivalent" to that offered in NYS schools. But this is only a legal argument, and not a moral one. [24]

If there is a moral principle that states that private schools must provide education substantially equivalent to that the state officials choose for New York government schools, then that is a good reason to impose effective penalties. But the educating interests of parents are diverse, and the educational interests of children can be satisfied in many different ways, so it is not clear why state officials in New York should impose substantial equivalence standards on private schools (and that's assuming we can make sense of the idea of substantial equivalence in the first place).

It is not as though New York state officials have special access to the truth about what a good education is. That is a matter of reasonable dispute and has typically been recognized as such. This is partly why the state has ignored the "substantial equivalence" standard for nearly a century and basically ignored what private schools do.

The second argument is that yeshivas receive a lot of indirect assistance from the public via taxpayer-funded welfare benefits. Here, YAFFED's argument is that it is the public's business how yeshiva students are educated because they receive taxpayer benefits, tax exemptions, and the like. But this principle would license enormous interference with the liberty of those who receive government support, much like aggressive drug testing for people who receive welfare benefits, or trying to control what people who receive Medicare eat to ensure that they are healthy, and do not take more public funds than necessary.

There are many interests that cannot be overridden simply by the fact that the public is paying for programs that promote those interests. However, in the case of the Haredim, they forgo a massive public service: public schooling itself, which in NYC costs more than $25,000 annually. It is doubtful that Haredi families are receiving welfare benefits in excess of $25,000. Therefore, neither of these arguments succeeds.

CONCLUSION

States may intervene into private religious school education under three conditions:

1. when the educational interests of children are significantly threatened and normally outweigh the educating interests of parents,
2. when the intervention is not excessively coercive or punitive, and
3. when the government has demonstrated its ability to secure the educational interests of children in these schools based on the history of their attempts to secure the educational interests of children in state schools.

But none of these conditions are clearly met in the case of the yeshiva system in New York State and New York City. Some yeshiva students do appear to have broken and inadequate English-language skills, but the data confirming this is weak, at best. Second, the proposed interventions are dramatic and disproportionate, arguably greatly in excess of what would be required to satisfy the educational interests of yeshiva students.

Finally, weaknesses in the New York State and New York City public school systems raise reasonable doubts about whether the relative coercive interventions would be effective at protecting or improving the educational interests of students. So in this dispute, the traditional liberal who embraces a presumption against state coercion and a default in favor of the liberty of parents, families, and communities should endorse the autonomy of yeshiva schools.

NOTES

1. Alisa Partlan et al., "Non-Equivalent: The State of Education in New York City's Hasidic Yeshivas," Young Advocates for Fair Education (Yaffed, Inc.) (2017), https://www.yaffed.org/report.

2. Stanley Benn, *A Theory of Freedom* (New York: Cambridge University Press, 1988), 112; Gerald Gaus, *The Order of Public Reason* (New York: Cambridge University Press, 2011), 341–46; Kevin Vallier, *Liberal Politics and Public Faith: Beyond Separation* (New York: Routledge, 2014), 30–31.

3. Loren Lomasky, *Persons, Rights, and the Moral Community* (New York: Oxford University Press, 1987), 152–87.

4. In cases of good faith disagreement about what is necessary for functional and flourishing childhoods, we tend to defer to parents and families, with limited oversight by states. It is hard to determine where the boundaries between state and civil society lie, and there is no space to pursue that issue in this essay.

5. And even Aramaic, though it is used primarily in Talmudic study and in liturgy.

6. Size is a matter of degree, so there is no threshold. But if you have more than a million language users, you're in the clear, unless the language is actually fake, like Klingon.

7. There are important gray areas in these standards, and reasonable people will disagree about the boundaries set out here. But we must balance what we would *like* students to know

and what we think is so important for children to know that we can override their parents' wishes. The aim is to strike a reasonable balance.

8. Girls also receive more religious training than the average student at a Christian religious school, though they spend half the day on secular subjects, while boys spend much less time on secular subjects.

9. Moshe Krakowski, "What Yeshiva Kids Are Actually Studying All Day," *The Forward*, December 26, 2018, https://forward.com/life/faith/416616/what-yeshiva-kids-are-actually-studying-all-day/. There is substantial diversity among the Haredim, it should be noted.

10. Partlan et al., "Non-Equivalent."

11. Agudah 2019 reports many of the concerns. See *The Yeshiva World*, "Yeshiva-Educated Education Professionals Reject Proposed NYSED Regulations," *The Yeshiva World*, 2019, https://www.theyeshivaworld.com/news/general/1781930/yeshiva-educated-education-professionals-reject-proposed-nysed-regulations.html.

12. New York State Education Department, "Substantial Equivalency," 2019b, http://www.nysed.gov/nonpublic-schools/substantial-equivalency.

13. Ryba v. Levy, N.Y. Slip Op. 30377 (N.Y. 2019).

14. Partlan et al., "Non-Equivalent."

15. Steve Lipman, "Yeshiva Probe Report Seen Inconclusive," *The New York Jewish Week*, August 21, 2018, https://jewishweek.timesofisrael.com/yeshiva-probe-report-seen-inconclusive/. Fifteen yeshivas were investigated, while the remaining fifteen refused investigators entry.

16. *Ryba.*

17. Partlan et al., "Non-Equivalent."

18. In addition, at one point, YAFFED insisted that NYS have a rule that no school district could credit what goes on in Jewish studies as course credit, but PEARLS prevailed in challenging any such rule and YAFFED didn't contest it.

19. There is significant disagreement within and among Orthodox communities as to what constitutes bitul Torah, but YAFFED does not differentiate between them and lacks the authority to make that determination.

20. It would also give the state the power to change the curriculum at other private schools that spend most of their days teaching secular subjects, which is why many of these groups also filed lawsuits against the DOE.

21. Richard Carranza, "Substantial Equivalence Inquiry," 6.

22. Partlan et al., "Non-Equivalent." Though there is evidence that yeshivas that teach secular subjects score among the top in NYS; Sandy Eller, "Regents Data: Public Schools Lag Behind Yeshivas," *The Jewish Press*, December 12, 2018, http://www.jewishpress.com/news/us-news/ny/regents-scores/2018/12/12/.

23. New York State Education Department, "New York State Education at a Glance," 2019a, https://data.nysed.gov/.

24. Moreover, this term has a morally dubious history, since it is rooted in nativist, anti-Catholic bigotry during the Know-Nothing era.

Chapter Two

Educational Pluralism

Distinctive Schools and Academic Accountability

Ashley Berner

How should democratic education systems balance individual rights and the common good?

Some theorists and practitioners reject the premise that we need to balance these values in the first place. Their objections often come from their two diametrically opposed directions: libertarians are prepared to fund parents to choose schools that match their values and let the selection process (or markets more generally) provide the accountability. By this logic, low-quality schools close of their own accord, as they are less frequently selected. The common-school movement supports the uniform delivery of education by the state, leaving space for individual beliefs to play out at home, on the weekends, and in church.

The libertarian model cedes little to the regulatory power of the state to enforce the common good. It portrays education as primarily about individual beliefs and community goals; any interference from political actors beyond nominal concerns—such as safety—grants inappropriate power to governmental authority. This position may be seen through the scholars highlighted in Kevin Currie-Knight's recent *Education and the Marketplace* (2019) and in policies that keep accountability measures to a minimum—such as Arizona's original tax credit program (1997) or Alaska's charter-school law (1995).[1]

The common-school position grants little to families besides the right to enroll one's child in a private school at personal expense. Here, the common good means a common educational experience, delivered exclusively by the state, in a space that attempts to transcend (or neutralize) the variety of viewpoints that exist within a plural society. This view is theorized by Amy

15

Gutmann, president of the University of Pennsylvania, and translates into the district-school-only bloc, whose adherents (such as Diane Ravitch and the National Education Association) resist the legitimacy of charter schools and private-school scholarship programs.

Between these positions is educational pluralism. Pluralists argue, with political scientist William Galston and educational theorist and historian Charles Glenn, that education belongs within civil society, subject to both individual and collective authority but controlled exclusively by neither. Educationally plural systems navigate this space by funding a wide variety of school models while requiring academic accountability for all of them. In other words, plural systems *separate the structure from the content of education*, leveraging the first to honor important differences, and the second to reinforce a (varied) level of educational commonality.

Below, I summarize the theoretical constructs of each position and set out why the pluralist model has distinct advantages over either a state-control or an individualist approach. I will assume, *per arguendo*, that all three models are put in place via democratic means, whether in the form of (elected) common-school legislatures in the late nineteenth century or (elected) school-choice legislatures in the twenty-first.[2]

Each model includes a spectrum of opinion; they are clustered together for clarity's sake. Each attempts to solve the same problem, namely, How does a democracy *most effectively and equitably* impart important knowledge, skills, and sensibilities to the next generation? None of the models solves all of the challenges associated with providing excellent and equitable education.[3] However, a well-crafted pluralist system offers maximum accommodation of individual and associational liberty and also a reasonable assurance of academic quality and democratic participation.

We begin with traditional political philosophy, which examines the relationship between the individual, the state, and civil society.[4]

In this chapter, "individual" refers to an independent and morally responsible human actor,[5] and the abstract "state" indicates the realm of governmental power. The notion of "civil society" as a distinctive sphere seems to have developed in the eighteenth century[6] and signifies the cluster of voluntary activities in which free citizens engage: the synagogue, the Rotary Club, philanthropies that support after-school programs and cancer research, local baseball leagues, and the community center.

Democratic political theorists do not dispute the importance of individual, state, and civil society, but disagree rather about their respective roles. How does this disagreement play out for education?[7] To be specific, how does the disagreement about roles implicate educational *structure, funding, accountability, and content*—the key decisions that must be made in designing and delivering democratic education? These four levers move sometimes in tandem, sometimes independently, as examples from school systems in the United States and around the world demonstrate.

THE ARGUMENT FOR STATE CONTROL

The argument for *exclusive state delivery of education* began as a strategy to manage diverse—and possibly divisive—populations. Canadian scholars Charles Taylor and Jocelyn Maclure call this approach "republican secularism,"[8] and Americans call it "civic republicanism."[9]

Civic republicanism emphasizes unity over difference and national over private interest; its adherents "desire for differences to be 'healed.'"[10] They expect the public square, and individuals who claim authority in the public square, to reflect nonparticularist values.[11] A private citizen may wear a Star of David, but a district judge may not. A Muslim may live out her faith freely in private and voluntary domains, but should not refer to the Koran in democratic debates. Public debate should be conducted in secular terms that match the secular state.[12]

The Netherlands, for instance, started out the nineteenth century with a highly heterogeneous population, many of whom had fled religious persecution elsewhere. Concerned about political disruptions born of deep differences, Parliament required attendance at state-run schools that imparted a "generally Christian," although widely perceived as deistic, philosophy.

The strategy did not work. In fact, it led to the secession of the (Catholic) southern provinces into a new country, Belgium.[13] The strategy, however, rests upon the claim that a state-controlled school system uniquely serves as a bridge between private and public lives and creates a neutral space where everyone can participate.

In the United States, Horace Mann, the chairman of the Massachusetts Board of Education (1837–1848), was an early champion of civic republicanism. Mann's priority was civic cohesion—something he did not believe schools with distinctive missions could accomplish. He argued that only state-controlled schools, the "common schools," could create the nondivisive preparation that young citizens required.[14] Note that this theory implicates both the structure and the content of education: both should be uniform, so as to create a common educative experience.

The most prominent contemporary theorists of state-controlled education are Amy Gutmann and Meira Levinson, who hold that the state is uniquely qualified to form democratic citizens and as such should fund, regulate, and exclusively deliver public education. Why? Because district schools derive from democratic processes and as such provide an important alternative to the nondemocratic institutions—such as the family or the church—that otherwise surround a child.[15]

District schools are designed explicitly to teach children how to speak in nonparticularist terms, the secular public language that is nonconfessional and shared by all. Gutmann refers to this key democratic skill, which is in essence a form of bilingualism, as "democratic deliberation."[16] Private schools also fall far short in this view; they are subject only to the will of parents, rather than to the judgment of the electorate.

What about the inevitable bureaucracy that many theorists describe as deleterious?[17] Gutmann agrees that bureaucratic excess harms schools, but in principle views numerous layers of governance as important representation of democratic government (local, state, federal), held in productive tension with the interests of teachers, families, and communities.[18] Gutmann further argues that district schools bring much-needed social capital to first-generation students, as well as connections between racial and socioeconomic groups.[19]

Meira Levinson goes still further, emphasizing that certain aims of democratic education—such as promoting individual autonomy—should not be open to democratic deliberation in the first place. Levinson writes:

> [f]or the state to foster children's development of autonomy requires coercion—i.e., it requires measures that prima facie violate the principles of freedom and choice. . . . The coercive nature of state promotion of the development of autonomy also means that children do not have the luxury of "opting out" of public autonomy—advancing opportunities in the same way that adults do.[20]

Levinson thus holds, as Charles Glenn summarized, that families ought not to withdraw from the state's education, nor should "this educational objective of autonomy itself be subject to public debate since . . . it is a fundamental premise of the liberal state which is not open to question."[21] Levinson's sophisticated defense of the common-school model concludes, logically, with a repudiation of private education and the suggestion of constitutional reform that would preclude its existence.[22]

Theories that undergird the state as sole provider of democratic schooling are thus well articulated and, thanks to America's long embrace of the common-school ideal, deeply embedded in cultural expectations about public education. The United States is not alone in embracing the common-school model, however; other uniform democratic school systems include Brazil, Greece, Jordan, Latvia, Mexico, the Philippines, and Uruguay. Some of these systems claim ideological neutrality (Mexico, Uruguay); others promote a religious standpoint (Greece, with right of withdrawal, or Jordan, which provides Islamic education).[23]

With respect to the four issues above (structure, content, funding, and accountability), the common-school model tends toward the following:

- *Structure* is uniform, i.e., public education is exclusively delivered by the state;
- *Funding* is for uniform schools, i.e., state funds flow only to schools managed by the state;
- *Accountability* (in whatever form) rests primarily with the state;
- *Content* is controlled variously.[24]

The last point is worth noting. Uniform systems sometimes require or incentivize a common curriculum for all students; others do not. The United States does not. Federal law prohibits a national curriculum, but even at the state level, the prescription of specific academic content has not been possible at scale (for many reasons) since the early twentieth century.[25] Research still shows variability within an individual district and even, and quite often, within a specific school.[26]

THE ARGUMENT FOR INDIVIDUAL RIGHTS

A libertarian theory of education stands at the opposite pole. This position interprets education as an individual or community good that should seldom be delivered by the state and never substantively regulated by it. As with the common-school model, the libertarian model encompasses a variety of voices.

Those at the far end of this spectrum suggest that the state should play no role in funding or providing public education. The English House of Lords, for instance, defeated a 1807 bill to raise taxes for the public education of low-income children on the grounds that parents and the voluntary sector should be in charge; low-income children should receive philanthropic grants to attend, if they attended at all.[27]

Parliamentary debates also reveal religious sectarian concerns that, if the state began to fund education, it would inevitably "fund error" (code word for the Anglican view of Catholic theology). Some twentieth-century American theorists agreed with noninterference. The economist Murray Rothbard (1926–1995), for instance, concluded that the oppression inherent in political institutions meant that democratic education should be noncompulsory and certainly not delivered by the state.[28]

By 1834 in England, and certainly by midcentury in developed nations, the state was seen as an important participant in preparing the next generation.[29] Libertarian thinkers offered important opposition, as Kevin Currie-Knight's *Education in the Marketplace: An Intellectual History of Pro-Market Libertarian Visions for Education in Twentieth-Century America* (2019) establishes in depth, albeit from a variety of positions rather than from a unitary perspective.[30]

For example, in the United States, Frank Chodorov (1887–1966) and Myron Lieberman (1919–2006) held that markets were superior to the state in providing democratic education. Both were suspicious of the political power that accrued to state actors;[31] both resisted state subsidies and state regulations; both viewed "consumer sovereignty" and competition as powerful mechanisms that would lead to continuous educational improvement.[32]

Market economists Rose and Milton Friedman (1910–2009; 1912–2002), for their part, focused on the positive consequences for neighborhoods and civil society (including racial integration) that they thought would flow from a market system. The Friedmans differed from some other prominent libertarians, like Rothbard and Chodorov, in supporting state-funded vouchers to this end, and state-provided education via district schools if necessary.[33] They also endorsed loose regulations of all schools (whether district or private).[34]

Fellow travelers, such as educational and civil rights activist Howard Fuller (1941–), interpret state accountability measures as merely the latest attempt by American policy makers to regulate and control families of color. Best, in Fuller's view, to provide state funding through which families of color might create their own schools, and regulate them as they see fit.[35]

A moderate example comes from Michael L. McConnell in his 2002 article, "Education Disestablishment: Why Democratic Values Are Ill-Served by Democratic Control of Schooling."[36] At first, McConnell sounds more like a pluralist than a libertarian.[37] As the pluralists, he argues that the mandate for free societies to prepare the next generation does not inevitably imply state control over the structure and content of education.[38] He argues (with pluralists) that a uniform delivery model inevitably offends the values of those outside of majoritarian norms.[39]

However, his "thin" approach to state oversight locates McConnell more firmly in the libertarian than the pluralist camp. He requests only that the state secure basic literacy and numeracy, and "perhaps minimal civic responsibility as well."[40]

> Beyond the scant essentials, a democratic society can let a thousand flowers bloom. There is no need for uniformity. The only need is for a modest form of regulation, to weed out those schools that do not even make an attempt to meet these basic democratic norms. Even then we should tread lightly; many a movement thought disturbing or abhorrent in its day turned out to make a positive contribution to American democratic culture.[41]

The role of the state is limited to "weed[ing] out schools" that "do not even make an attempt" at literacy and numeracy. Given the intellectually low bar that has characterized American education for so long,[42] one wonders how many schools would actually find themselves defunded, and by what criteria. Indeed, it is difficult to see how even modest academic skills might be enforceable in McConnell's schema, since he repeatedly notes that pedagogical approach and the selection of content are contingent upon core values.[43]

As we will see, pluralists endorse academic accountability—as long as it does not trespass upon a school's distinctive ethos.

With respect to the four issues above (structure, content, funding, and accountability), therefore, the libertarian model tends toward the following:

- *Structure* is plural, i.e., the state does not exclusively deliver public education—and in some libertarian views, should not deliver it at all;
- *Funding* is student-centered, i.e., state or even exclusively private money follows the child (via tax credits, vouchers, education savings accounts);
- *Accountability* resides primarily with parents, not with the state, although the state should ensure basic safety and health, and fundamentals of literacy and numeracy;
- *Content* should be determined at the parental and school level.

In other words, the libertarian position is to enable a panoply of school types to exist (through state or private funding) and to provide them with maximal freedom to enact the wishes of families. The market processes, exercised primarily through enrollment decisions, constitute the most important lever over academic and civic quality.

THE PLURALIST ARGUMENT: DIFFERENTIATED STRUCTURE, COMMON ACCOUNTABILITY

Liberal pluralism seeks a balance between the individual, the state, and civil society. It shies away from absolutizing any one institution—whether individual, state, or voluntary organization. As political philosopher James Skillen put it, principled pluralism seeks "to avoid or overcome the absolutization of the family, the state, the market, and the individual in order to promote societal differentiation and integration."[44]

The pluralist theory of education developed historically in parallel with the common-school theorists. I noted earlier that the Netherlands began the nineteenth century with a state-control model and ended it with a pluralistic one. Theorizing *why* a state-control model was inadequate to the task of educating an increasingly democratic nation played an important role in the process. As Charles Glenn explains, both Protestant and Catholic leaders relativized the state *and the individual* theoretically and thus created space for distinctive schools located within the domain of civil society.[45]

Protestants did so by drawing upon the notion of "sphere sovereignty," and Catholics, "subsidiarity." Sphere sovereignty asserts that the voluntary associations of society, whether the press, the church, the family, or the arts, possess inherent dignity that derives from their own (not the state's) purpose and should be honored with meaningful responsibility.

The state's proper role is minimal and consists solely of "mediat[ing] among these 'spheres,' ensuring that justice is done, the rights of individuals are protected, and that tasks that can only be undertaken by the whole society are carried out."[46] The state should prevent abuse and exercise appropriate, if limited, regulations. However, the state should not intervene in the texture of familial life, the conduct of business, or the relationship between a pupil and a teacher.[47]

Catholic leaders drew upon the theological notion of "subsidiarity," or the "ethical principle that a larger and higher ranking body should not exercise functions which could be efficiently carried out by a smaller and lesser body; rather the former should support the latter by aiding it in the coordination of its activities with those of the greater community."[48] That is, the smallest unit capable of executing a social function should do so.[49]

It follows from both theories that the state should not hold the exclusive rights to provide public education. In real-world terms, the argument led to the Netherlands' expansive pluralism in which the state funds thirty-six different kinds of schools on equal footing.

A more recent theory of pluralism is William Galston's *Liberal Pluralism* (2002). Galston sets out a democratic theory that balances individual (and associational) rights with those of the state and, in education, the state's imperative to produce democratically apt citizens. Galston pushes back against the common-school model and suggests a "parsimonious" use of state power in defining and cultivating citizenship in young students.[50] Why?

First, Galston notes the particularity—in this case, an Enlightenment rationalism and preference for individualist autonomy—of Gutmann's and Levinson's accounts.[51] The values of autonomy and deliberation are worthy goals, he writes, but they represent only one of many ways to understand the human condition, the good life, and even democratic society.[52] Thus, a decision by the state to restrict funding to only schools that advance autonomy "side[s] with the ultimate claims of one group and not others."[53]

Instead of promoting one view of the world and preparing children for it, as common-school theorists want, "the value-pluralist liberal state will respect self-aware, autonomous lives but will not insist on promoting Socratic or Millian ideals (or any others) as valid for all citizens."[54] Rather, it will accommodate the beliefs of Catholics, Jews, and Evangelical Christians (for instance) in public institutions generally and schools in particular.

Galston further disputes Gutmann's view that democracy requires citizens to bracket their belief systems in the public square. The goal of bilingualism, in which children learn the language of faith or ideology at home and that of "public reason" at school, begs the question of whether a neutral public discourse can exist, or should. Far better, Galston writes, to help students learn to articulate their political views *and the derivation of those views* in the public square. Only in this way can a diverse population come to understand their fellow citizens, "clash imaginatively," and come to affect one another over time. [55]

Finally, he points out, a uniform education simply cannot exhaust the civic goods that we want our schools to promote. The Amish, advocates of Waldorf education, or Protestant homeschoolers, for instance, might not endorse an Enlightenment version of democratic deliberation, but their communities and schools might nurture other civic virtues—such as "law-abidingness, personal and family responsibility, and tolerance of social diversity"[56]—goods that an individualist approach does not cultivate, except perhaps by accident.

In the pluralist view, therefore, state-controlled education imposes upon minority viewpoints and unevenly nurtures democratic culture.[57] But this engages with the structure, not the content, of public education. How do pluralists stand on this issue? In contrast to the majority of libertarians, pluralists favor accountability to the state with respect to academic outcomes.

The premise is that democracy requires a knowledgeable citizenry. Since the late eighteenth and early nineteenth centuries, democratic governments have rested their case for public funding for education here.

Whether we review England's first national resolution for government funding for education (1833),[58] then-Governor Thomas Jefferson's *Bill for the More General Diffusion of Knowledge* (1797),[59] *Brown v. Board of Education's* magisterial language (1954),[60] or the federal government's National Commission on Excellence in Education ("A Nation at Risk"—1983), we find the call to create a common, democratic culture. In the latter's words, "A high level of shared education is essential to a free, democratic society and to the fostering of a common culture, especially in a country that prides itself on pluralism and individual freedom."[61]

What constitutes the "shared education" and "common culture," though? For America's founders, a liberal arts education. Jefferson was quite certain that a democratic education should include robust knowledge of history, politics, English literature, mathematics, and science, and build the capacities of skillful writing and public oratory. Benjamin Franklin, Benjamin Rush, and George Washington agreed with this intellectual scope.[62]

As Diane Ravitch and E. D. Hirsch have noted, however, American education departed from this norm of intellectual formation a hundred years ago.[63] This fact renders Americans less equipped to impart the domains of history, politics, English literature, math, and science that Jefferson thought would equalize opportunities and create an educated citizenry. With some notable exceptions, America's schools rely upon the inculcation of generic skills rather than specific academic content—to the detriment of citizenship formation and opportunity.[64]

Most democratic school systems, by contrast, still require a liberal arts curriculum, which is assessed uniformly across distinctive schools. Alberta, Canada, for instance, funds Catholic, Protestant, Inuit, and home education (to name a few) and requires robust assessments based upon common academic standards and content.[65]

Many OECD countries even require that students take courses on comparative religion and ethics, every year, in all schools—another key insight that democratic citizenship requires knowledge of how other people—even within one's own society—think and believe.[66] Such requirements echo Galston's earlier point about the civic value of enabling cultural and religious minorities to offer the "fact" of their beliefs to the public square. Practice needs to start in the classroom.

Plural systems attempt to honor individuals' values and advance the common good *by distinguishing between school culture and academic content*. Plural systems promote the distinctive values of different schools and also require the impartation of publicly shared academic content through the schools—or what Charles Glenn calls "education and instruction."

> The good school that engages with settled intention to provide both effective instruction and character-forming education to the pupils entrusted to it by their parents is thus accountable both to society in general and to families though along different dimensions of its mission. Society, through government, has every right to require adequate instructional outcomes so as to ensure that every child has a fair opportunity in life. It is not society's right, however, to prescribe the *educational* dimensions of the school's mission: how it shapes the character and convictions of its pupils. That, in a pluralistic democracy, is for parents to determine by their choice of schools.[67]

There are, of course, nuances in policies—such as the Netherlands' funding of creationist schools while requiring that students learn about the theory of evolution, or Waldorf schools opting out of the Netherlands' generous provision of funds because they are not willing to administer the state's written exams. My colleague Charles Glenn sets out many of these nuances in chapter 6 of this volume.

With respect to the four issues above (structure, content, funding, and accountability): the pluralist model tends toward:

- *Structure* is plural, i.e., the state does not exclusively deliver public education;
- *Funding* is plural but contingent, i.e., state monies are widely distributed to schools who comply with the state's accountability structure;
- *Accountability* resides with the state, i.e., the state establishes academic and civic benchmarks;
- *Content* is not necessarily prescribed, but often is.

With respect to the United States, as mentioned, accountability for nondistrict schools exists on a spectrum, with Louisiana on the "tight," and Arizona on the "loose," ends. Intellectual content is only rarely prescribed by the state, nor are content-based assessments required—even of district schools. The extent to which the state *should* specify academic content, and if so, on what basis (Hours of instruction? End-of-course assessments?), is the focus of this volume.

CONCLUSION

Democratic political philosophy assumes the importance of the individual, the state, and the voluntary sector, but assigns different roles to each. As represented by Amy Gutmann and Meira Levinson, the common-school model maximizes the role of the state in funding and regulating schools; in many democracies, this also includes prescribing the content of education. The libertarian model maximizes the role of the family and civil society in the funding, structure, and content, while the state largely withdraws.

William Galston's liberal pluralism and Charles Glenn's structural pluralism, by contrast, argue for diversity of school types—and funding to ensure it—contingent upon the willingness of distinctive schools to submit to the state's academic and civic oversight. In many democracies, this includes the expectation that all funded schools deliver a common body of knowledge.

Educational pluralism poses challenges for the United States. In its acceptance of funding of distinctive schools, educational pluralism pushes against the cultural norm of uniformity. In its acceptance of state accountability that may include common curricula and assessments, and site visits, it pushes against the individualism that Americans—and private-school families—prize.

Certainly, educational pluralism solves some problems but creates new ones;[68] even historically plural school systems have tensions around each of the four key decisions about structure, funding, accountability, and content. When we look around the world, however, we find that the pluralistic approach often yields impressive academic and civic outcomes. It certainly offers a lot to our fractured public square.

What does the framework of educational pluralism bring to the yeshiva controversy? At the point of writing, the accuracy of the claims against the yeshivas has not been validated, nor the response of New York State finalized. Broadly speaking, however, a pluralist perspective would affirm both the value of distinctive schools such as the yeshivas and also the obligation of the state to ensure a minimum standard of secular education.

NOTES

1. National Alliance for Public Charter Schools, "Measuring Up to the Model: A Ranking of State Public Charter Laws" (Washington, DC: National Alliance for Public Charter Schools, January 2019), https://www.publichcarters.org/ranking-state-public-charter-school-laws-2019; Glen Y. Wilson, "The Equity Impact of Arizona's Tax Credit Program: A Review of the First Three Years (1998–2000)," Research Report (Tempe: Arizona State University, March 2002).

2. An important qualification, indicated below, is Meira Levinson's claim that the fundamental goal of democratic education is not subject to democratic debate.

3. Advocates of each position acknowledge as much. See, for instance, chapter 6 in Ashley Berner, *Pluralism and American Public Education: No One Way to Go to School* (New York: Palgrave Macmillan, 2017).

4. In this chapter I use the term "state" generally, meaning any level of governmental authority.

5. This is a general term that is not intended to diminish those circumstances in which particular individuals, for mental or cognitive reasons, are deemed not to be morally responsible for their behavior.

6. Boris deWiel, "A Conceptual History of Civil Society: From Greek Beginnings to the End of Marx," *Past Imperfect* 6 (1997): 5.

7. Chapter 3 in Berner, *Pluralism and American Public Education*, provides much more detail on this subject.

8. Jocelyn Maclure and Charles Taylor, *Secularism and Freedom of Conscience*, trans. Jane Marie Todd (Cambridge: Harvard University Press, 2011).

9. This is not to be confused with the civic republicanism (or civic humanism) described and debated by J. G. A. Pocock and Thomas Pangle in J. G. A. (John Greville Agard) Pocock, *Politics, Language, and Time: Essays on Political Thought and History* (Chicago: University of Chicago Press, 1989), and Thomas L. Pangle, *The Spirit of Modern Republicanism: The Moral Vision of the American Founders and the Philosophy of Locke* (Chicago: University of Chicago Press, 1988). It is, rather, the civic republicanism promoted by Benjamin Rush and George Washington—a common and nondenominational piety that sought public virtue, as described in John Witte Jr. and Joel A. Nichols, *Religion and the American Constitutional Experiment*, fourth ed. (Oxford: Oxford University Press, 2016), 36–42.

10. Kathleen Knight Abowitz and Jason Harnish, "Contemporary Discourses of Citizenship," *Review of Education Research* 76, no. 4 (December 1, 2006): 657–59.

11. One must note, of course, that "nonparticularist" is still particularist. In nineteenth-century America, the Protestant majority thought of itself as nonparticularist; today, many secular elites think of themselves the same way.

12. I explore this tension in chapter 6, in the context of religious schools and Quebec's provincial curriculum, in *Pluralism and American Public Education.*

13. This narrative is chronicled beautifully in Charles L. Glenn, *Contrasting Models of State and School: A Comparative History Study of Parental Choice and State Control*, first ed. (New York: Continuum, 2011); Charles L. Glenn, *The Myth of the Common School* (Amherst: University of Massachusetts Press, 1988).

14. The classic book on this subject is Glenn, *The Myth of the Common School.*

15. Amy Gutmann, *Democratic Education* (Princeton: Princeton University Press, 1987): 30–32, 48.

16. Gutmann follows John Rawls in seeking out a universally accessible public discourse. Rawls's work on this subject (see especially John Rawls, "The Idea of an Overlapping Consensus," *Oxford Journal of Legal Studies* 7, no. 1 [1987]: 1–25; John Rawls, "The Idea of Public Reason," in *Deliberative Democracy: Essays on Reason and Politics*, eds. James Bohman and William Rehg [Cambridge: MIT Press, 1997]: 93–145), led to a rich discussion among political theorists about whether his ideal was attainable or desirable. See, for example, Mark Button, "Arendt, Rawls, and Public Reason," *Social Theory and Practice* 31, no. 2 (2005): 257–80; Marc Stears and Mathew Humphrey, "Public Reason and Political Action: Justifying Citizen Behavior in Actually Existing Democracies," *The Review of Politics* 74, no. 2 (2012): 285–306; and Jurgen Habermas, "Reconciliation Through the Public Use of Reason: Remarks on John

Rawls's Political Liberalism," *The Journal of Philosophy* 92, no. 3 (1995): 109–31, https://doi.org/10.2307/2940842, on Rawls's broader liberal framework.

17. E.g., John E. Chubb and Terry M. Moe, *Politics, Markets, and America's Schools* (Washington, DC: Brookings Institution, 1990), https://www.brookings.edu/book/politics-markets-and-americas-schools/.

18. Gutmann, *Democratic Education*, 70, 74, 297. Note, however, that Gutmann is not sanguine about the negative impact of *too much* bureaucracy. She supports slimming down extraneous bureaucratic mandates but not, in principle, the structures themselves.

19. Gutmann, 30–32. The empirical record on this matter is discussed elsewhere within this volume.

20. Meira Levinson, *The Demands of Liberal Education* (Oxford: Oxford University Press, 2002), 38–39, 139. Cited in Charles L. Glenn, "Structural Pluralism in Education: Can We Stop Fighting Over Schools?," *Johns Hopkins Institute for Education Policy* (blog), December 15, 2017, http://edpolicy.education.jhu.edu/wp-content/uploads/2017/12/Structuralpluralism.pdf.

21. Glenn, "Structural Pluralism," with reference to Levinson, *The Demands of Liberal Education*, 38–39, 139.

22. Levinson, *The Demands of Liberal Education*, 161–63.

23. See summary in Ashley Berner, "Funding Schools," in *Balancing Freedom, Autonomy, and Accountability in Education*, eds. Charles Glenn and Jan De Groof, vol. 1 (Tilburg: Wolf Legal Publishers, 2012), 115–29, and full descriptions in Mahasen M. Aljaghoub, "Jordan," in *Balancing Freedom, Autonomy, and Accountability in Education*, eds. Charles Glenn and Jan De Groof, vol. 3 (Tilburg: Wolf Legal Publishers, 2012), 243–54; Nina Ranieri, "Brazil," in *Balancing Freedom, Autonomy, and Accountability in Education*, eds. Charles Glenn and Jan De Groof, vol. 3 (Tilburg: Wolf Legal Publishers, 2012), 61–78; Vasiliki Apostolopoulou, "Greece," in *Balancing Freedom, Autonomy, and Accountability in Education*, eds. Charles Glenn and Jan De Groof, vol. 2 (Tilburg: Wolf Legal Publishers, 2012), 229–44; Edvins Danovskis, "Latvia," in *Balancing Freedom, Autonomy, and Accountability in Education*, eds. Charles Glenn and Jan De Groof, vol. 2 (Tilburg: Wolf Legal Publishers, 2012), 277–88; Rosa Elena Teran Morales and Jorge Alberto Mahecha Rodriguez, "Mexico," in *Balancing Freedom, Autonomy, and Accountability in Education*, eds. Charles Glenn and Jan De Groof, vol. 3 (Tilburg: Wolf Legal Publishers, 2012), 255–66; Vivien M. Talisayon, "Philippines," in *Balancing Freedom, Autonomy, and Accountability in Education*, eds. Charles Glenn and Jan De Groof, vol. 3 (Tilburg: Wolf Legal Publishers, 2012), 287–98; Pablo Landoni, Charles Glenn, and Jan De Groof, "Uruguay," in *Balancing Freedom, Autonomy, and Accountability in Education*, eds. Charles Glenn and Jan De Groof, vol. 3 (Tilburg: Wolf Legal Publishers, 2012), 397–415. It must be acknowledged, of course, that the democratic nature of Jordan's government is disputed.

24. The curriculum, and thus the intellectual content, used in American classrooms varies considerably. See footnote below.

25. The reasons for this are numerous; they include a bias toward skills over content; resistance on the grounds of local control; and the inevitable political disputes that arise from the selection of specific content. See, for instance, E. D. Hirsch, *The Schools We Need: And Why We Don't Have Them* (New York: Doubleday, 1999); E. D. Hirsch, *The Making of Americans: Democracy and Our Schools* (New Haven: Yale University Press, 2009); Diane Ravitch, *Left Back: A Century of Battles Over School Reform* (New York: Simon & Schuster, 2001); Robert K. Fullinwider, *Public Education in a Multicultural Society: Policy, Theory, Critique* (Cambridge; New York: Cambridge University Press, 1996). This is not to say that incentivizing high-quality curricular materials does not occur. See, for instance, Julia Kaufman, Lindsay Thompson, and V. Darleen Opfer, "Creating a Coherent System to Support Instruction Aligned with State Standards: Promising Practices of the Louisiana Department of Education" (Arlington: The Rand Corporation, September 2016), http://www.rand.org/content/dam/rand/pubs/research_reports/RR1600/RR1613/RAND_RR1613.pdf; Johns Hopkins Institute for Education Policy, "Using the RFP Process to Drive High-Quality Curriculum: Findings from the Field," Policy Brief (Baltimore: Johns Hopkins Institute for Education Policy, October 2018), http://edpolicy.education.jhu.edu/wp-content/uploads/2018/10/RFP.pdf.

26. V. Darleen Opfer, Julia Kaufman, and Lindsay Thompson, "Implementation of K-12 State Standards for Mathematics and English Language Arts and Literacy: Findings from the American Teacher Panel" (Santa Monica: The Rand Corporation, 2016), https://www.rand.org/content/dam/rand/pubs/research_reports/RR1500/RR1529-1/RAND_RR1529-1.pdf. The Johns Hopkins Institute for Education Policy has repeated this survey across the country and found similar results. James Murphy, *Church, State and Schools in Britain, 1800–1970* (London, UK: Routledge & K. Paul, 1971): 4.

27. James Murphy, *Church, State and Schools in Britain*, 4.

28. Kevin Currie-Knight, *Education in the Marketplace: An Intellectual History of Pro-Market Libertarian Visions for Education in Twentieth Century America* (New York: Palgrave Macmillan, 2019).

29. For details, see Ashley Berner, "Metaphysics in Educational Theory: Educational Philosophy and Teacher Training in England (1839–1944)" (D.Phil. diss., University of Oxford, 2008), or J. A. Roebuck, "National Education," Hansard § Volume XX (1833), http://hansard.millbanksystems.com/commons/1833/jul/30/national-education.

30. Currie-Knight, *Education in the Marketplace*.

31. Ibid., 43.

32. Ibid., 53, 147.

33. Ibid., 113–19. Currie-Knight describes the evolution of the Friedmans' thought, influenced by E. G. West, toward supporting the ultimate abolition of government involvement in education, except possibly for the very poor, though they continued to support universal vouchers over means-tested vouchers so long as there were government-run schools.

34. Milton Friedman, "The Role of Government in Education," in *Economics and the Public Interest*, ed. Robert A. Solo (New Brunswick: Rutgers University Press, 1955): 123–44.

35. Howard Fuller, "Advancement—The Second 'A' in NAACP—Should Apply to Our Children Too," *The 74 Million* (blog), August 2, 2017, https://www.the74million.org/article/howard-fuller-advancement-the-second-a-in-naacp-should-apply-to-our-children-too; Howard Fuller, "Call It 'Ed Reform' or Don't—The Fight to Make Schools Work for Our Poorest Families Must Go On. To Stop Is to Dishonor King's Memory," *The 74 Million* (blog), January 17, 2019, https://www.the74million.org/article/fuller-call-it-ed-reform-or-dont-the-fight-to-make-schools-work-for-our-poorest-families-must-go-on-to-stop-is-to-dishonor-kings-memory; Derrell Bradford, Chris Stewart, and Howard Fuller, "Liberating Black Kids from Broken Schools—By Any Means Necessary," *The 74 Million* (blog), June 26, 2017, https://www.the74million.org/article/bradford-fuller-stewart-liberating-black-kids-from-broken-schools-by-any-means-necessary.

36. David Steiner, "The Ethics of Education Policies," in *The Routledge Handbook of Ethics and Public Policy*, eds. Annabelle Lever and Andrei Poama, Routledge Handbooks in Applied Ethics (Routledge, 2018): 156–65. Both McConnell and my colleague David Steiner place McConnell in the pluralist camp. With respect, I disagree, for the reasons above.

37. Indeed, he self-identifies as a pluralist.

38. Michael W. McConnell, "Education Disestablishment: Why Democratic Values Are Ill-Served by Democratic Control of Schooling," *Nomos* 43 (2002): 99.

39. Ibid., 96.

40. Ibid., 88.

41. Ibid., 103.

42. Eric A. Hanushek, Paul Peterson, and Ludger Woessman, "Not Just the Problems of Other People's Children: U.S. Student Performance in Global Perspective" (Boston: Harvard's Program on Educational Policy and Governance and *Education Next*, May 2014), https://sites.hks.harvard.edu/pepg/PDF/Papers/PEPG14-01_NotJust.pdf.

43. McConnell, "Education Disestablishment," 102–3.

44. James W. Skillen, *In Pursuit of Justice: Christian-Democratic Explorations* (Lanham: Rowman & Littlefield, 2004): 30.

45. See Glenn, *Contrasting Models of State and School*, for an excellent account of the development of the Netherlands' school system.

46. Ibid., 130, 131.

47. Ibid., 131.

48. Domènec Melé, "Exploring the Principle of Subsidiarity in Organizational Forms," *Journal of Business Ethics* 60, no. 3 (2005): 293.

49. Subsidiarity was reflected in a papal encyclical on the just society. See Pope Leo XIII, "Rerum Novarum: On Capital and Labor" (Papal Encyclical, May 15, 1891), http://www.papalencyclicals.net/Leo13/l13rerum.htm. See sections 49–59 on associations. It is also a cornerstone of European human rights law. See Paolo Wright-Carozza, "Subsidiarity as a Structural Principle of International Human Rights Law," *American Journal of International Law* 971, no. 2003 (2003): 38–79.

50. William A. Galston, *Liberal Pluralism: The Implications of Value Pluralism for Political Theory and Practice* (Cambridge; New York: Cambridge University Press, 2002), 20, http://dx.doi.org/10.1017/CBO9780511613579.

51. Ibid., 21, 107.

52. Ibid., 95.

53. Ibid., 20.

54. Ibid., 62.

55. Ibid., 101, 115.

56. Ibid., 107.

57. Galston also disputes the unique capacity of district schools to bestow moral and social capital. The empirical record is discussed in chapter 4 of Berner, *Pluralism and American Public Education* and in Elmer John Thiessen, *Teaching for Commitment: Liberal Education, Indoctrination, and Christian Nurture* (Montreal; Buffalo; Leominster: McGill-Queen's University Press, 1993), 89.

58. Roebuck, "National Education."

59. Thomas Jefferson, "79. A bill for the more general diffusion of knowledge, 18 June 1779" (1779), http://founders.archives.gov/documents/Jefferson/01-02-02-0132-0004-0079.

60. Oliver Brown, Mrs. Richard Lawton, Mrs. Sadie Emmanuel, et al. v. Board of Education of Topeka, 347 United States Reports 483 (U.S. 1954).

61. National Commission on Excellence in Education, "A Nation at Risk: The Imperative for Educational Reform," Evaluative Reports; Policy Guidance (Washington, DC: U.S. GPO, 1983), http://www2.ed.gov/pubs/NatAtRisk/risk.html.

62. Lorraine Smith Pangle and Thomas Pangle, "What the American Founders Have to Teach Us about Schooling for Democratic Citizenship," in *Rediscovering the Democratic Purposes of Education*, eds. Lorraine M. McDonnell, P. Michael Timpane, and Roger Benjamin (Lawrence: University Press of Kansas, 2000).

63. Ravitch, *Left Back*; Hirsch, *The Making of Americans.*

64. E. D. Hirsch, *The Knowledge Deficit: Closing the Shocking Education Gap for American Children* (Boston: Houghton Mifflin, 2016).

65. Amy von Heyking, "Alberta, Canada: How Curriculum and Assessments Work in a Plural School System" (Baltimore: Johns Hopkins Institute for Education Policy, June 2019), http://edpolicy.education.jhu.edu/wp-content/uploads/2019/06/Alberta-Brief.pdf. Note that the state can trespass upon values in the process of requiring specific content; see, for instance, a discussion of Quebec's Ethics and Religious Culture curriculum in Berner, *Pluralism and American Public Education*, 110–11; Stephen Prothero, *Religious Literacy: What Every American Needs to Know—And Doesn't* (New York: HarperCollins, 2007).

66. Stephen Prothero, *Religious Literacy.*

67. Glenn, "Structural Pluralism."

68. I explore many of these tensions in chapter 6 of *Pluralism and American Public Education.*

Chapter Three

Pork Eating Is *Not* a Reasonable Way of Life

Yeshiva Education versus Liberal Educational Theory

Rita Koganzon

1. PORK EATING AS A REASONABLE WAY OF LIFE

Before the Hasidic Jews of New York, there were the Amish of Wisconsin. William Galston called them the "model case" in the long-running debate over religious diversity in liberal regimes.[1] Not being liberal themselves, they nonetheless posed little threat to the liberal state and wanted primarily to be left alone by it. As a result, for the past nearly fifty years, the Amish have lived a kind of shadow life in political theory as avatars of the problem of tolerating the intolerant, and especially for the problem of tolerating the children of the intolerant.

The near-simultaneity of John Rawls's publication of *A Theory of Justice* (1971) and the U.S. Supreme Court's decision in *Wisconsin v. Yoder* (1972) made this strange life possible. The threat to Rawlsian liberalism posed by *Yoder* was that of resurgent religious fundamentalism and theocracy. The Amish sought only a narrow exemption from Wisconsin's compulsory schooling law, but after Reagan's election in 1980, the relatively innocuous and few Amish came to represent the more menacing and substantially larger group of evangelicals. What if the exemption from schooling granted to the Amish were to be exploited by evangelicals on a much larger scale?

Rawls argued that justice did not generally require toleration of the intolerant, but "there is no reason to deny freedom to the intolerant" unless the tolerant "sincerely and with reason believe that their own security and that of the institutions of liberty are in danger."[2]

31

What reason is sufficient to believe this? *Yoder* raised precisely this question. Does private religious education endanger liberty, at least for the children receiving it, and perhaps even for the whole state? The fear of incipient theocracy is reflected in the conclusions of much of the Rawlsian argument, which aimed to constrain the ability of religious parents to pass their religious faith on to their children.[3]

The linchpin of these arguments was that parents' efforts to instill their religious beliefs in children through education undermined the children's future *autonomy*, which it is the duty of the liberal state to protect. This protection entails securing each child's "right to an open future" or his capacity to weigh and revise conceptions of a good life or "choose among a range of good lives."[4] Where Kant had originally understood autonomy as the capacity to legislate the moral law to oneself, liberal educational theorists defined it down to mean something like the capacity to change one's mind. Such revision almost universally required broad "exposure to diversity" in education to enable autonomous choices.[5]

Although the exposure requirement permits parents to *privilege* their own way of life, it prohibits them from *excluding* other possibilities from their children's upbringing, or as Gutmann put it: "Parents certainly have a right . . . to forbid their children to eat pork within their home, even though they also have a duty to allow their children to be exposed to the knowledge that eating pork is considered a reasonable way of life by many other people."[6] An education that shields children from such exposure to reasonable pork eating forecloses their future autonomy to choose pork eating for themselves and thereby violates liberal principles of justice.

The practical or policy demand of the Rawlsian argument was uniform public schooling for all, and the prohibition—or at least radical circumscription—of private schooling. Meira Levinson, for example, requires private schools to be open to all and to avoid teaching "fundamental" or "socially divisive" conceptions of the good, effectively prohibiting religious schooling and rendering private schools indistinguishable from public ones, which "is as it should be."[7] Matthew Clayton similarly denies that parents have any right to educate children "according to principles that . . . depend upon controversial beliefs about religion."[8]

Other theorists worried that the outright suppression of religious education would provoke dangerous resistance, so proposed instead that private school curricula be closely regulated. This would ensure that they "teach the common set of democratic values," which include "religious toleration, mutual respect among races, and the cognitive skills necessary for ensuring all children an adequate education," and that they provide sufficient "exposure to diversity" to permit autonomous choice.[9]

A half-century on from Rawls and *Yoder*, the constellation of threats to civic health has surely changed. It should now be clear, if it wasn't then, that the fear of theocracy arising from parental control of education was over-blown. Educational reforms from the 1980s on have given parents more educational control than ever, deregulating schooling and legalizing home-schools, charter schools, online schools, and other alternatives. Self-reported religious affiliation (especially evangelical Protestant affiliation) has declined substantially over the same period. [10]

The narrow sectarian indoctrination of evangelical children that liberal theorists feared never came to pass. But the Rawlsian argument constructed against it has remained the dominant approach to understanding the respective roles of the state, parents, and children in education. [11] Compelled exposure to pork eating as a reasonable way of life is still the goal.

THE RAWLSIAN ARGUMENT AND THE YESHIVAS

Today, the New York yeshiva controversy offers a new "model case" to reconsider the liberal argument in light of political circumstances that have changed substantially since the Amish came to stand in for all religious dissenters from secular liberalism. Yeshiva education poses in some ways a more serious challenge to mainstream society than the Amish claim, but it is also a more typical challenge in the twenty-first century.

The pastoral way of life of the Amish is archaic but not foreign. It preserves two deeply rooted American ideals: the independent yeoman farmer and the pious Christian. One of the key points of Justice Burger's defense of the Amish in *Yoder* was that they were an economically self-sufficient community, and their agricultural training qualified them for paid work outside the sect, should they choose to leave it.

Hasidic Jews offer neither of these reassurances. Although Judaism has a long history in the United States, it has never occupied a central place here, and the way of life that Hasidism elevates—lifelong study of religious texts—is not a deeply rooted American ideal. Hasidic Jews also make no strong claim to communal self-sufficiency. They are socially insular and engage in extensive private social service provision, but they live in dense and diverse urban and suburban communities and participate in local economies and governments, including as recipients of public benefits.

Hasidic Jews do not offer modern Americans an image of themselves at the nation's founding, as the Amish did in 1972. They have more in common with the kinds of dissent from secular liberalism that we see more often now—from immigrants, including non-Western immigrants, and Catholics. Relatively integrated into the modern economy, these groups ask not to be left alone by the state, but to receive benefits from it without conceding to its demands for religious neutrality.

The Amish have stood apart from American modernity in a relatively static way for a century, remaining not only socially and economically separate but even legally exempt from its demands. Hasidic Jews are, by contrast, embedded in modernity and changing along with the secular society of which they are a part, though they remain visibly distinct from that society.

We are now in a reasonable position to ask whether liberal theory's fifty-year-old devotion to compulsory and centralized public education grounded on exposure to diversity and the promotion of autonomy as open-ended choice is really suitable to the preservation of liberal regimes. The 1980s and 1990s fear of Christian theocracy can no longer reasonably motivate our considerations when so many of those asking for consideration are not Christians, and are so few in number that they plainly pose no political threat to the majority.

At the same time, new political threats have surfaced. Numerous studies have called attention to the polarization of American society along socioeconomic and subsequently partisan lines, and to the growth not just of economic inequality, but of alienation and its attendant social pathologies, like crime, family dissolution, and drug abuse, which had otherwise been declining across the country.[12]

The vast majority of those affected by this decline are products of American public education.[13] They are mostly secular.[14] Whether their educations actually made them autonomous is difficult to empirically test, but we have every reason to assume that their public schools promoted autonomy to the extent that they were able, and exposed them to a variety of ways of life, including pork eating.[15] Yet none of this seems to have brought them much in the way of widespread flourishing and political cohesion.

The Rawlsian argument is certainly not to blame for these outcomes, but it did not do much to alleviate them either. The "autonomy" that liberal education has aimed at has not helped those at the bottom of the socioeconomic ladder in the United States to live better or more fulfilling lives, not just in terms of earnings but in terms of personal flourishing. It likely hasn't helped most of those at the top either, but its failures there have been less visible, or more easily obscured by the benefits of wealth.

At the same time, among Americans with lower levels of educational attainment and income, some groups do not exhibit anywhere near the same levels of social distress as the secular mainstream. The traditional religious communities that liberal theory has had so much difficulty accounting for, like the Amish and now the Hasidim (along with newer immigrant groups that exhibit lower but still significant levels of religious observance), have managed to avoid many of these scourges. They exhibit low rates of crime, drug addiction, and other social pathologies.[16] The Hasidic way of life may strike most Americans as undesirable, but as far as we can empirically discern, they are better off in body and soul than many of their secularly educated counterparts.

This new political context, in which liberalism finds itself competing for the loyalties of a large, alienated working class and battling illiberal ideologies that had seemed moribund during the heyday of Rawlsian theorizing, ought to motivate a better approach to our thinking about the rights of parents, children, and the state in education.

In the past, yeshiva education would likely have been condemned even by those liberal theorists most sympathetic to religious education for neglecting even to ensure students' fluency in English.[17] At best, it would have been tolerated only under increased state oversight.

But our present political situation may offer an opportunity to reconsider why communities like the Hasidim seem to be able to avoid some of the negative outcomes that afflict similarly poor groups, and to consider whether educations like those offered by the yeshivas are not only negatively defensible on the grounds that they do not harm the regime, but positively contribute to the cultivation of virtues and ways of life that fortify liberalism against the allure of rival regimes.

3. THE UNREASONABLENESS OF PORK EATING AS A WAY OF LIFE

There are two fundamental reasons that the Rawlsian argument fails to address the challenges presently facing liberalism. First, although the autonomy aimed at by liberal education purports to give children a neutral and broad selection of lives, it is neither neutral nor broad in reality, but highly normative and narrow. Second, although childhood exposure to diversity is intended to expand our liberty and capacity for independent thought as adults, it actually undermines the development of the very virtues necessary to exercise such independence.

The effectual result of a Rawlsian education is, on one hand, the moral elevation of an elite, cosmopolitan educational and professional trajectory above more attainable and rooted ways of life, and on the other, the deprioritization of the virtues of commitment, constancy, and self-control in a regime most in need of extra support for these virtues.

In its strongest form, the first objection—that an education for autonomy is not a neutral foundation upon which the child can stand to rationally adjudicate among competing worldviews, but a normative worldview in itself—would delegitimize practically any state education.[18] But even if we accept that liberal regimes *should* predispose children to favor liberalism, this objection nonetheless usefully alerts us to the sometimes-hidden normativity of all education.

In the case of Rawlsian education, this normativity goes farther than simply elevating liberalism above other regimes. Its conception of autonomy as open-ended choosing elevates the secular, upwardly mobile professional who can succeed in a globalized economy. Such people appear maximally autonomous because they have access to the greatest number of lifestyle choices available in contemporary America, among the greatest variety of careers, hobbies, friends and potential spouses, residences, and consumer goods. A successful education for an open future is actually an education for this particular kind of professional future.

An education that aims at an open future does expand certain kinds of particularly consumption-oriented options, but it quietly closes off certain other production-oriented choices. It makes it harder to justify pursuing a manual trade, for example, since the training for such a trade sacrifices some liberal education to narrower vocational training and closes off many possible futures. A college degree is a flexible and transferable qualification, allowing one to choose among many careers and even to change careers in accordance with one's changing conception of the good. A plumbing apprenticeship only trains and qualifies its holder for one specific line of work, and this narrowing of future options is a problem even if that line of work would be more fulfilling to its recipient than college education.

It is also difficult to justify, on autonomy grounds, turning down opportunities for professional advancement and increased income in order to do things like remain in one's hometown or take care of one's family. Liberal theory does not outright condemn these decisions, just as it doesn't prohibit people from becoming plumbers, but it can't endorse them either, since they all limit the variety of available choices and consequently constrain the capacity to revise one's way of life. As feminist critics have also shown, elevating autonomy means diminishing and denying all kinds of lives and choices—and not exclusively religious ones—that do not maximize personal agency and freedom from external constraint.[19]

The second reason Rawlsian theory is ill-suited to the present is its limited ability to cultivate the virtues most necessary to sustain liberalism itself. Preparing children for an open future requires us to prevent them from making the choice to stop choosing and actually adhere to something. Liberal education aims to *detach* religious children from their parents' worldviews so that they are able to critically examine and revise them, but it could never *attach* a secular child to such worldviews, since one cannot autonomously select a way of life that demands that he give up choosing for himself in essential matters.[20]

Consequently, the kind of religious faith that liberalism permits must always be superficial and contingent. But the imperative and expectation of constantly changing one's deepest moral commitments stunts the development of one of the most necessary virtues for liberal regimes—that of self-control, which is developed by *commitment* to principles and persistence in them rather than their perpetual reconsideration and abandonment.[21]

The virtues that come from being brought up in a serious and demanding faith like Hasidic Judaism and choosing to remain in it are rarely considered by liberal theorists. This decision does not even clearly appear as a choice to them, since it is externally indistinguishable from heteronymous submission to authority.

By contrast, the individual who spends his life picking up and discarding ways of life like faddish diets in a restless quest for the most satisfying one may be the perfect picture of autonomy, since he has amply demonstrated the ability to critically revise his view of the good. But surely it is a problem for liberal regimes if their ideal citizen is fickle, distracted, and lacks the will-power to pursue even what he autonomously chooses. How then can he adhere even to liberal principles?[22]

At the same time as Rawlsian education weakens the child's self-control, or at least fails to strengthen it, liberal societies present him with what Callan calls "the autonomy-destroying pressures of popular culture."[23] The world beyond the public school (and often within it) is rarely one of "edifying ethical pluralism." Television and social media, books, music, and peers, embodied and virtual, are decisive for the development of character and values, and the values that they espouse are not always very salutary. Exposing children to diversity without any anchoring principles to discriminate among the competing lives that this diversity holds out risks simply surrendering them, unarmed, to vapid consumerism and "polymorphous nihilism."[24]

If eating pork and not eating pork are both reasonable ways of life, how do we choose? Liberal theory has no answer where neither choice causes harm. But the child needs answers about the best way of life, and a negative standard like the harm principle does not suffice.

Absent authoritative guidance from parents or teachers, the child will either make his choices on mere whim, or find other, perhaps less salutary authorities who are less skittish about comprehensive worldviews, to guide his choices. Without a well-developed capacity for self-control, how will he stand up to the seductions from both his own uncontrolled desires, and from society's?

Early liberal philosophers of education like John Locke and Jean-Jacques Rousseau recognized the significance of this threat from popular culture, or what they called "opinion" and "fashion," and for that very reason made the development of self-control the central purpose of their pedagogies.[25] The danger that public opinion poses comes not from the particular opinions that it supports or rejects, but from its ability to implant in individuals an unshakable desire to conform to it in order to be held in esteem.

Even if schools taught perfectly correct and rational ideas, children would still come away from them morally weakened from the experience of subjection to the collective authority of their peers. Self-control, they argued, could only come from the consistent application of a singular source of authority during childhood that could strengthen the child's will against his desires, or keep the desires themselves at bay.[26]

Both thinkers consequently warned against schooling because of the peer pressure and conformism that always comes with groups of children.[27] "They want to bring you down to their low level, and they reproach you for letting yourself be governed [by your tutor] only in order to govern you themselves," Emile's tutor tells him when he encounters the fashionably vulgar boys of Paris. "To set themselves above the alleged prejudices of their fathers, they enslave themselves to those of their comrades."[28]

For early liberals, it was counterintuitively an insular and authoritarian education at home that provided the essential foundation for freedom. The differences between the way of life in the family and that of the larger society, heightened by the insularity developed from protecting children from outside influence, would provide all the exposure to diversity that a child would need to understand that there are competing visions of the good life, and to induce him to consider, at the appropriate age, whether his parents have really got it right. This entirely organic exposure to diversity, inevitable in any liberal regime, requires no coercive supplementation by state institutions.

Unlike contemporary liberals, who see almost all the danger in education arising from "indoctrination" by the family, early liberals saw little to fear in the family's influence over the child. They understood that the family was only one of many influences vying for the child's loyalty, and especially given the legal restrictions on it in a liberal state (from liberalized inheritance laws and a uniform age of majority), it would be one of the weakest.

Exposure to diversity at this age would only have the effect of introducing many competing desires and authorities to please that the child could neither adjudicate among nor satisfy on his own. This confusion would weaken his will at the point when it was just developing. Contemporary liberals assume that parental influence is enormously effective, so that by the end of education, it will be so deep-rooted as to be permanent and unshakable. But early liberals worried about its very *weakness* in the face of competing pressures, particularly Callan's "autonomy-destroying pressures of popular culture."[29]

4. PORK EATING VERSUS VIRTUE

Universal homeschooling is not a practical possibility in modern democratic societies where most parents must work for a living, but parent-controlled religious education offers a close approximation of its benefits. Although it still suffers from the defects of schooling about which early liberals worried, such an education nonetheless engages in two practices that they saw as essential to freedom. First, it sets the child against the mainstream culture and works assiduously to protect him from it until adulthood. Second, because it rejects the pedagogical inclination to democratize and diminish the authority of adults that plagues liberal theory, it sets the child under the consistent and relatively harmonious authority of parents, teachers, and in this case also a rabbinical tradition going back two thousand years.

Such schooling creates conditions under which self-control can be developed. This virtue of self-control is highly transferable—more so even than an elite liberal arts degree—since it supports both a life of continued piety, or any kind of satisfying life in secular society for those who choose to leave their religious upbringings behind.

This authoritarian/protective structure is shared by many religious schools, but the content of yeshiva education is unusual in a relevant way. Liberal theorists often worry that traditional religious education consists of memorization and passive absorption of dogmas, leaving no room for students to develop their own critical capacities.[30] The pedagogy of the yeshiva, however, is dialectical. Textual study is undertaken in pairs and consists of translation and discussion of passages of the Torah and Talmud and other commentaries. Students analyze texts, often in the original ancient language (Hebrew or Aramaic), and dispute their interpretation with each other and their teachers.

Moshe Krakowski has pointed out that this "more closely resemble[s] upper-level humanities coursework in a university than clerical training or contemplation of the Divine," and we might add that it is closer to university work than even the secular school curriculum, which still rests largely on passive absorption.[31]

Yeshivas thus combine authority and protection with disputation and criticism, simultaneously cultivating self-control and the critical capacity necessary for liberal citizenship. This combination is all but absent in liberal theory, which tends to view all authority as an obstruction to the equality and liberty that children ought to learn in school.

However intellectually advanced it may be, perhaps yeshiva education may still be faulted for its narrowness and failure to prepare children even for economic and civic duties within the Hasidic community, no less those beyond it. But this criticism both overstates how much of education takes place in school and underestimates the influences that crowd in from outside.[32]

It is hard to imagine that there is a Hasidic adolescent in America who is unaware that there is another way of life, one that includes pork eating and is overwhelmingly more popular than his own, abroad in the land. There is little reason to impose such exposure along with Gutmann's insistence that pork eating is "reasonable." This we can safely allow him to determine for himself. He is exposed to diversity simply by virtue of being an extreme minority, as is true of all traditionally religious citizens of liberal societies.

The Hasidic adolescent is also in a stronger position to seriously engage with diversity than the secular one who is exposed to a superficial parade of possibilities that hardly challenge his own weakly rooted preconceptions very deeply. He has not a naive personal preference but a two-thousand-year-old tradition to weigh against the alternatives. He must also weigh the serious social and economic consequences of resisting the secular mainstream against the deep disapproval of his family and community if he joins it. These are very high stakes, especially for the young, and they add seriousness and urgency to the encounter with diversity that the secular child, who faces no serious consequences for selecting one possibility over another, does not experience.

We might finally ask whether the open and autonomous life of the secular professional that liberal theory elevates ought to be the standard to which all education should be "substantially equivalent," as New York's statutory language has it. This kind of education protects an open future above all else, but it is a future so open as to be essentially empty. Its only aim is to avoid closure. In this respect, it is not actually more practical or preparatory for the "real world" than yeshiva education.[33]

Lifelong experimentation and revision of one's conception of the good means, in practice, a great deal of instability, including in those spheres where stability is most essential for success, like family and career. For those without extensive financial resources to cushion and offset radical changes in family and work arrangements, such instability can be financially and personally devastating. Rawlsian educational theory is not, consequently, essentially democratic. Both its personal and financial costs and its hoped-for outcome of robust autonomy make it attainable only by a few.

In effect, liberal theory has valorized a kind of education that only a small elite can well afford—not simply financially, but more importantly, psychically—because it is designed to weaken, in the name of autonomy, the sorts of commitments—to family, religion, and place—that anchor life for the vast majority of citizens.

Hasidic education, like most traditional religious education in the tight-knit communities that persist in the United States, does precisely the opposite. It encourages these commitments, and commitment itself (as the virtue of self-control), which in turn improve life for individuals and communities, even under the relatively impoverished economic conditions that have eroded social capital in other communities in the country.

5. KASHRUT IS A REASONABLE WAY OF LIFE

In the polarized political climate of the early twenty-first century, liberal democracies are at risk of capitulating to illiberal political philosophies unless they can address the problems of alienation and despair, family disruption, unemployment, and the erosion of community. An education that can do this without coercion or violation of the basic rights that the liberal state guarantees is, in effect, liberal, whether or not it aims at or achieves autonomy or an open future for each child.

This is true even if that education is religious. Indeed, given the rather poor outcomes of the past thirty years of liberal educational theory, it may be time to consider whether *preventing* children from receiving religious upbringings is at odds with liberalism, rather than vice versa.

The original aim of liberal education was not to squash religion, but to cultivate virtue, and particularly the virtue of self-control. Early liberals thought this could best be done in the insularity of the family, by ceding all authority to parents to educate their children in a way that would protect them from the moral distortions of "fashion" or popular culture.

Modern conditions do not permit such education on a large scale, but schools can approximate this goal by helping religious parents to impart their ways of life to their children, not because these ways of life are themselves liberal, but because they are an antidote against Callan's "polymorphous nihilism" during an especially critical developmental moment. Every educational input need not be liberal in order for the result to be liberal, as the early liberals who envisioned authoritarian childhoods as the precondition of free adulthoods understood.

That is not to say, of course, that everyone should send their children to Hasidic yeshivas. Coerced religious education is no better than coerced secularism. However, the substantial number of non-Catholic parents in search of alternatives to public school who have sent their children to Catholic schools should prevent us from dismissing out of hand the appeal of religious schooling for nonreligious ends. [34]

But for the yeshivas, this only means that their approach merits the consideration of liberal theorists and the respect of the liberal state, unless it is in direct violation of the basic right of all students to a physically safe learning environment and an eventual right of exit from the community if such exit is desired.

Nor does this mean that the state should subsidize sectarian education, directly or even indirectly (as it currently does). The problem here is, again, not one of permanent principle, since in principle if religious education is better at inculcating virtue, it might merit state support. It is merely practical, since in a state that protects diversity, it will be even more difficult than elsewhere to adjudicate among all the potential applicants for aid, and the possibility of funding will encourage rent-seeking and other forms of corruption.

But the state should not reflexively turn away from religious education. Liberal theorists have forgotten that "Properly understood, liberalism is about the protection of diversity, not the valorization of choice."[35] It was, at its inception, designed to protect religion by undermining the domination of any single church. The legal protection of religious minorities was always in keeping with that end, while the promotion of autonomy was only ever a private aim for the few, not a state purpose.[36]

At a time when liberal regimes across the world seem to be floundering and failing to provide opportunities for basic human flourishing of perhaps half of their citizens, it is imperative that we reconsider the flattened proceduralism and complacency of Rawlsian theory. Liberalism is not a self-powering machine consisting of a static set of cogs—institutions and beliefs—that, if only arranged correctly, will guarantee its permanent reproduction. It is a much looser and more dynamic regime, always in competition and contact with both antiliberal and nonliberal ways of life. It can refute the antiliberal alternatives, but it can also co-opt the nonliberal ones, using some of their strengths to buttress its own weakness.

One of its greatest weaknesses is the difficulty of cultivating the kind of self-discipline necessary to sustain a relatively noncoercive government under prevailing conditions of immense openness and choice, of teaching its citizens to govern themselves so that the state does not have to step in and do it for them. Contemporary liberal theorists have largely taken this capacity for granted (and actually undermined it by proposing to teach children how to manage openness and choice by simply forcing more of it on them), but early liberals worried a great deal about where it would come from once traditional authorities and constraints were abolished.

The past half-century has shown us that one promising source is traditional families and religious observance. Groups who maintain what we might call preliberal or premodern ways of life like Hasidic Jews (and the Amish, and so on) are not just acceptable but may be essential for liberal democracy to preserve.[37]

Although the logical appeal of congruence is strong, liberalism need not be totalizing or remake every institution within society in its image to be successful. It can easily afford to maintain alternatives to itself within itself, both as outlets for individuals who simply cannot be satisfied with what liberalism has to offer, and as moral buttresses for those who are. A decentralized educational landscape where parents can control their children's educations and impart demanding, comprehensive worldviews is not a threat to liberalism's continuity. But a flattened, uniform one that takes the lives of academic philosophers to be the universal standard to which all education should aspire, and something as facile as exposure to pork eating as a reasonable way of life as its most serious moral demand, may well be.

NOTES

1. William A. Galston, "Two Concepts of Liberalism," *Ethics* 105 (1995): 518.
2. John Rawls, *A Theory of Justice* (Cambridge: Harvard University Press, 2009), 192–93.
3. This fear is explicitly voiced by Amy Gutmann in "Children, Paternalism, and Education," *Philosophy and Public Affairs* 9 (1980): 348, and Stephen Macedo, *Diversity and Distrust* (Cambridge: Harvard University Press, 2000), 153–65. It is implicit in the writings of almost all Rawlsian theorists of education.
4. I am flattening some of the subtleties here by eliding somewhat different aims under the banner of autonomy, but I take Meira Levinson's point that even those theorists who claim to be arguing for less than autonomy ultimately depend on it. See Levinson, *The Demands of Liberal Education* (Oxford: Oxford University Press, 1999), ch. 2. The origin of the open future argument is Joel Feinberg's "The Child's Right to an Open Future," in *Whose Child?*, eds. William Aiken and Hugh LaFollette (Lanham: Rowman & Littlefield, 1980), 124–53. Other autonomy arguments range from the most maximalist in, e.g., Levinson, *The Demands of Liberal Education*, Eamonn Callan, *Creating Citizens: Political Education and Liberal Democracy* (Oxford: Oxford University Press, 1997), and Matthew Clayton, *Justice and Legitimacy in Upbringing* (Oxford: Oxford University Press, 2006), to less demanding ones like Gutmann's *Democratic Education* and Macedo's *Diversity and Distrust*.
5. Macedo, *Diversity and Distrust*, 202–3; Jeff Spinner-Halev, "Extending Diversity: Religion in Public and Private Education," in *Citizenship in Diverse Societies*, eds. Will Kymlicka and Wayne Norman (Oxford: Oxford University Press, 2000), 75–76.
6. Gutmann, "Children, Paternalism, and Education," 353.
7. Levinson, *Demands of Liberal Education*, 145, 157. Paradoxically, religious schools are only permissible in societies where religion is *not* taken seriously.
8. Clayton, *Justice and Legitimacy*, 3.
9. Gutmann, *Democratic Education*, 117–18; Macedo, *Diversity and Distrust*, 202–3. See also Callan, *Creating Citizens*, 190–92.
10. See Gallup's historical polling on religious observance, 1948–2018: https://news.gallup.com/poll/1690/religion.aspx.
11. Examples of recent work on religious families and education that remains oriented around the imperative of autonomy and grounded in the old debate include, for example, Clayton, *Justice and Legitimacy in Upbringing*; Harry Brighouse and Adam Swift, *Family Values* (Princeton: Princeton University Press, 2009); Randall Curren and J. C. Blokhuis, "The Prima Facie Case against Homeschooling," *Public Affairs Quarterly* 25 (2011): 1–19; Ian McMullen, *Faith in Schools?* (Princeton: Princeton University Press, 2007).
12. June Carbone and Naomi Cahn, *Marriage Markets: How Inequality Is Remaking the American Family* (Oxford: Oxford University Press, 2014); Charles Murray, *Coming Apart: The State of White America, 1960–2010* (New York: Crown Forum, 2013); Robert Putnam, *Our Kids: The American Dream in Crisis* (New York: Simon & Schuster, 2015).
13. Ninety percent of children attend public schools and more than 95 percent of low-income children do, a proportion that has held steady since the 1970s. Richard J. Murnane, Sean F. Reardon, Preeya P. Mbekeani, and Anne Lamb, "Who Goes to Private School," *Education Next* 18, no. 4 (Fall 2018).
14. Murray, *Coming Apart*, 204–12; Putnam, *Our Kids*, 223–26.
15. We can't know how many teachers have been consciously motivated by Rawlsian principles, but we can examine their general political leanings. A 2017 study found that American schoolteachers self-identified as broadly center-left, with only 27 percent identifying as Republicans. An earlier meta-analysis of GSS data from 1972 to 2006 found teachers to be more liberal than the general population, but slightly more conservative than those with equivalent education. Holly Yettick, Sterling Lloyd, Alexandra Harwin, and Michael Osher, "Educator

Political Perceptions: A National Survey," *Education Week Research Center*, December 2017; Robert Slater, "American Teachers: What Values Do They Hold?," *Education Next* 8, no. 1 (Winter 2008).

16. Reliable social statistics about Orthodox Jewish communities are only beginning to be gathered by the Orthodox Union, but some rough and indirect clues can be obtained from data from areas home to majority Hasidic populations. Brooklyn's Borough Park, for example, is ranked by crime statistics aggregator DNAInfo as the third-safest neighborhood in New York City, while its neighbor to the east, Flatbush, and the more expensive Park Slope to the north, rank fortieth and forty-first respectively (https://www.dnainfo.com/new-york/crime-safety-report/ranking/). Rockland County, which is home to several Hasidic towns and villages, has a much lower crime rate than any comparably dense county in New York State. New York State Crime Report, 2017 Preliminary Data, https://www.criminaljustice.ny.gov/crimnet/ojsa/Crime-in-NYS-2017-Preliminary-5-10-18.pdf. Census data from the towns of Monsey, Kaser, and New Square indicate a married family household rate between 92 and 97 percent, compared with 78 and 74 percent in the nearby non-Hasidic but affluent suburban towns of West Nyack and Croton-on-Hudson. The difference is even starker when compared to comparably poor and similarly sized upstate locations like Middleton, which has a married household rate of only 65 percent. U.S. Census, Community Facts, https://factfinder.census.gov/faces/nav/jsf/pages/community_facts.xhtml.

17. If yeshiva critics are correct about their failure to offer any secular education, they likely violate even a minimal requirement like Galston's for "the development of 'social rationality.'" Galston, "Two Concepts," 525.

18. This is the version articulated by Nomi Stolzenberg, "'He Drew a Circle That Shut Me Out': Assimilation, Indoctrination, and the Paradox of Liberal Education," *Harvard Law Review* 106 (1993), 581–667. She argues that the Rawlsian argument rests on a rationalistic epistemology that is fundamentally at odds with certain religious ways of understanding the world as, for example, divinely ordered in ways not amenable to rational explanation. Such rationalism is incompatible with faith, and what liberals take to be mere "exposure" to a way of life is actually indoctrination into a worldview that forecloses faith. Liberalism on this view is a kind of antireligious religion blind to its own bias.

19. E.g., Martha Nussbaum, "The Feminist Critique of Liberalism," Lindley Lecture, University of Kansas, 1997.

20. Spinner-Halev, "Extending Diversity," 76. Spinner-Halev says this most explicitly: "[Autonomous people] will come to justify their way of life, or *more likely they will change their way of life*, sometimes in large ways and sometimes in small ways, as they encounter different ways of living and different ideas" (emphasis added).

21. Callan, "Autonomy, Child-Rearing, and Good Lives," in *The Moral and Political Status of Children*, eds. David Archard and Colin M. Macleod (Oxford: Oxford University Press, 2002), 134. As Callan has put it in an essay that he admits constitutes a reconsideration of his earlier work, "The excessive preoccupation with protecting the conditions for autonomous revision to the good . . . obscures the equal importance of autonomous adherence."

22. Geoffrey Vaughan, "The Overreach of Political Education and Liberalism's Philosopher-Democrat," *Polity* 37, no. 3 (July 2005): 389–408. Vaughan points out that autonomy is not tied to any particular regime and could easily entail the rejection of liberalism itself.

23. Callan, "Autonomy, Child-Rearing, and Good Lives," 139.

24. Ibid., 135–36. Some liberal theorists like Spinner-Halev ("Extending Diversity") and Robert Noggle have tried to deal with this objection by dividing up childhood: they allow parents to instill "value systems" in early childhood so that the child may be grounded in some tradition (seemingly any will do for this purpose), but then require criticism of this tradition during adolescence. Thus Noggle, for example, admits that "we cannot give the child a completely open future by making her present free of any values or any metaphysical or religious doctrines," but still insists that parents have no right to "make the child close-minded with regard to other value systems or world-views." Noggle, "Special Agents: Children's Autonomy and Parental Authority," in *The Moral and Political Status of Children*, eds. David Archard and Colin M. Macleod (Oxford: Oxford University Press), 114–15. But an arbitrary introduction to

a tradition that is contradicted later on by the same people who offered it is the weakest of antidotes against Callan's "polymorphous nihilism."

25. John Locke referred to self-control by a variety of names in *Some Thoughts Concerning Education*—"mastery" or "dominion" over the self, or "self-denial"—but it is the central virtue of his pedagogy: "He that has not a mastery over his inclinations, he that knows not how to resist the importunity of present pleasure or pain, for the sake of what reason tells him is fit to be done, wants the true principle of virtue and industry, and is in danger of never being good for anything" (*Some Thoughts*, §45). Jean-Jacques Rousseau similarly concludes that "the virtuous man . . . is he who knows how to conquer his affections." *Emile: Or, On Education*, trans. Allan Bloom (New York: Basic Books, 1979), 443–44.

26. Locke preferred the first approach and Rousseau the second. On Locke and the education of the will, see Rita Koganzon, "'Contesting the Empire of Habit': Habituation and Liberty in Lockean Education," *American Political Science Review* 110 (2016): 547–58. Among contemporary scholars, a similar argument has been advanced by Shelley Burtt, "In Defense of Yoder: Parental Authority and the Public Schools," *Nomos* 38 (1996), 425.

27. Locke, *Some Thoughts*, §70; Rousseau, *Emile*, 49, 330, 388.

28. Rousseau, *Emile*, 330–32.

29. Even relatively incompetent parents will be more benevolent primary authorities for moral development than the authority of fashion and opinion, so long as they are not outright neglectful. Neither thinker considered the possibility of absolutely fanatical parents, but both assumed seriously religious ones. Rousseau was explicitly forgiving of unenlightened or otherwise subpar parents, arguing that "zeal will make up for talent better than talent for zeal" in familial education (*Emile*, 48). Locke also "accepted a measure of illiberal sentiment in the parents in exchange for the positive contribution made by the concern that they supplied." Richard Ruderman and R. Kenneth Godwin, "Liberalism and Parental Control of Education," *The Review of Politics* 62 (2000): 512–13.

30. E.g., Spinner-Halev, "Extending Diversity," 78.

31. Moshe Krakowski, "What Yeshiva Kids Are Actually Studying All Day," *The Forward*, December 26, 2018, https://forward.com/life/faith/416616/what-yeshiva-kids-are-actually-studying-all-day/.

32. Burtt, "In Defense of Yoder," 426.

33. Ironically, many elements of secular education are valued precisely for their impracticality. The study of the classics, for example, is one well-regarded, even aspirational, element of an open, liberal education. It is substantively very similar to yeshiva training, consisting entirely of textual analysis in ancient languages, and yet few liberals wish to prohibit it for failing to impart civic or economic skills.

34. "Non-Catholic student enrollment has risen from 2.7% in 1970 to 11.2% a decade later and today is 19.0%." See "Catholic School Data: Enrollment," National Catholic Education Association, 2019, https://www.ncea.org/NCEA/Proclaim/Catholic_School_Data/Enrollment_and_Staffing/NCEA/Proclaim/Catholic_School_Data/Enrollment_and_Staffing.aspx?hkey=84d498b0-08c2-4c29-8697-9903b35db89b.

35. Galston, "Two Concepts of Liberalism," 523.

36. Even Locke thought that most people were incapable of freeing their minds from the habits of deference to received opinion and the craving for social esteem that encouraged such deference.

37. This would not apply to communities and ways of life that are not peaceful, or whose purpose is to destroy the liberal regime hosting them. Dissenting communities must make their peace with the majority among whom they live as well and use the common mechanisms of electoral politics and government to achieve their public ends. The point here is not that ISIS deserves state protection.

Part Two

Religious Liberty and Education Law

Chapter Four

State Regulation of Curriculum in Private Religious School

A Constitutional Analysis

Aaron Saiger

All private schools in New York State are required by law to provide "instruction . . . substantially equivalent to the instruction given" in nearby public schools. The statute further requires New York public schools—the schools to which the nonpublic schools must be "substantially equivalent"—to provide a course of study through the eighth grade that includes "the twelve common school branches of arithmetic, reading, spelling, writing, the English language, geography, United States history, civics, hygiene, physical training, the history of New York state and science." The code requires a similar course of study for high schools. [1]

Several graduates of Haredi boys' yeshivas recently alleged that their and similar schools provide egregiously minimal or even no secular instruction, sending graduates into the world illiterate in English, incompetent at basic arithmetic, and with no exposure to the sciences, secular history, or civics. [2]

When these allegations reached the New York State Department of Education, it decided, after an investigation, [3] to enforce the statutory requirement of "substantial equivalence" much more rigorously. In a reversal of previous practice, the department also announced that it would subject all private schools, including yeshivas, to regular compliance reviews.

The yeshivas naturally object to the heightened enforcement. More fundamentally, they assert that any obligation to devote a substantial portion of the school day to secular instruction is inimical to their mission and their faith. Haredi Judaism demands intensive religious instruction, a demanding task for which every hour is precious. That task, they claim, requires the bulk of every school day. No more than a few hours of the day can be sacrificed for secular study, certainly nowhere near enough time to cover the state's laundry list of required subjects.

Although the particulars of this dispute are idiosyncratic, the fundamental legal question it raises is neither parochial nor pedestrian. It involves two fundamental and competing constitutional principles. On one side, federal and state constitutions in the United States assign to the states both the power and the duty to educate children within their borders.[4] On the other, those same constitutions guarantee the freedom of conscience and thought generally, and free religious exercise in particular. The controversy over the yeshiva curriculum places these principles in direct conflict.

This chapter focuses on the constitutional dimension of the dispute. It asks: Suppose a yeshiva were to demur to the most serious allegations that have been made, and assert a constitutional right to educate its students with minimal secular instruction, or even no secular study whatsoever. What is the constitutional validity of such an assertion?

Two basic constitutional arguments could be made in its favor. The first invokes liberty: families must be permitted the freedom to raise and educate their children according to their particular preferences. Instead, or in addition, eschewing secular subjects might be a matter of freedom of religion. In lawyers' nomenclature, the first of these is a claim of substantive due process rights under the Fourteenth Amendment. The second is a free exercise claim under the First Amendment.

After considering the Fourteenth and First Amendment arguments in turn, this chapter concludes that the state has the better of both. States may constitutionally require private religious schools to provide a robust program of secular instruction. Such demands cannot be so extensive as to commandeer all or nearly all of the private school day. But New York's statute, and its enforcement by the Department of Education, fall short of transgressing that limitation.

LIBERTY AND THE PRIVATE SCHOOL CURRICULUM

The Due Process Clause limits the extent and character of state efforts to regulate private education. Three cases about private schools, decided by the Supreme Court in quick succession in the 1920s, together establish several basic propositions. They are:

1. Compulsory education is constitutional.
2. Parents have a constitutional right to refuse public education, but those who exercise that right can be required to secure private education instead, at their own expense.

3. The state may regulate private schools for public purposes.
4. Any such regulation of private education may not be so intrusive that it forces a private school to behave as if it were a public school, rendering it unable to carry out its particular educational mission. [5]

The second of these cases to be decided, *Pierce v. Society of Sisters*, is the most famous of the three. [6] The case nullified an Oregon statute that required parents of children between the ages of eight and sixteen to send their children to a public school. [7] Justice McReynolds wrote in *Pierce* that pursuant to the guarantee of liberty in the Due Process Clause, a state has no "general power" to "standardize its children by forcing them to accept instruction from public teachers only." [8] *Pierce* thus establishes a constitutional right to private education.

The other two cases applied the same principle to statutes that, rather than prohibiting private schools outright, imposed onerous regulation upon them. *Meyer v. Nebraska*, decided in 1923, invalidated a Nebraska law that prohibited private and public schools alike from teaching a foreign language to students who had not completed the eighth grade. [9]

Farrington v. Tokushige, decided in 1927, similarly invalidated a Hawaii statute that imposed arduous conditions upon any "school which is conducted in any language other than the English language or Hawaiian language, except Sabbath schools." [10] The law required such "foreign language schools" to obtain annual permits and allowed the territory to dictate what courses would be taught, what textbooks would be used, when the schools could operate, and which students were allowed to attend. [11]

Meyer and *Farrington*, like *Pierce*, emphasized that the restrictions at issue were unconstitutional because they interfered with a parent's ability to "direct the education of his own child without unreasonable restriction." [12]

Meyer and *Farrington* establish that the federal Constitution prohibits not only a ban on private schooling, but also regulatory regimes that hobble them. At the same time, however, the 1920s cases make it clear that some kinds of regulation, including fairly demanding kinds, are constitutionally permissible. *Meyer* states that "the power of the State to compel attendance at some school and to make reasonable regulations for all schools, including a requirement that they shall give instructions in English, is not questioned." [13] *Pierce* contains similar language:

> No question is raised concerning the power of the State reasonably to regulate all schools, to inspect, supervise and examine them, their teachers and pupils; to require that all children of proper age attend some school, that teachers shall be of good moral character and patriotic disposition, that certain studies plainly essential to good citizenship must be taught, and that nothing be taught which is manifestly inimical to the public welfare. [14]

This permits private school regulation to "do much [and] go very far, indeed."[15] As the Supreme Court restated the doctrine in 1976, parents' right to secure private education is not a right to educate their children "unfettered by reasonable government regulation."[16] But to be constitutional, regulation must be "reasonable." Whether affirmative curricular obligations imposed upon private schools are constitutional is therefore a line-drawing question. There is no set maximum quantum of obligation that the state may impose.

The important limitation upon affirmative regulation is that it may not demand so much time as to make it impossible for private schools to do anything of their own choosing. This is why the rules in *Farrington* are invalid, for example. A regulation that demands that all or nearly all of the time available be devoted to compliance with state rules is not permitted.[17]

The power of the state to regulate private-school curricula up to a point is justified by its interest in an educated populace. The state is interested both to prevent people from being public charges (an issue discussed in the next section) and to ensure that they can competently participate as citizens in the economy and the polity. Courts often cite in particular that all persons need to be able to cast informed votes and to serve intelligently on juries.[18]

So—setting aside for now the free exercise claim discussed in the next section—states can constitutionally demand that private schools not eschew all secular teaching. Moreover, the state may demand instruction in particular topics. There is specific constitutional authority for states to demand instruction in several topics required by New York and alleged to be omitted from the yeshiva curriculum, notably the English language, mathematics, science, and civics.[19] Instruction in English (but not instruction *exclusively* in English) has been singled out by the U.S. Supreme Court as a permissible requirement.[20]

Indeed, a strong case can be made that all of the twelve topics included in the New York statute's "course of study" provisions for middle schools—the weakest case, it seems to me, is the "history of New York state"—are sufficiently necessary to effective life and citizenship that they can constitutionally be demanded. They are also constitutional if demanded together, subject to the above-noted rule that the state may not affirmatively regulate so heavily that the private school has no time to further its private purposes. This would be to "standardize" children.[21]

FREE EXERCISE AND RELIGIOUS SCHOOL CURRICULA

The yeshivas are not just private schools; they are religious schools. Although both *Meyer* and *Pierce* involved church schools, the 1920s cases rested entirely on the Due Process Clause. They made no particular claims about religion. It was not until the 1970s that the Supreme Court considered whether the First Amendment right to free exercise of religion necessitated a religious exemption from compulsory schooling.[22]

In *Wisconsin v. Yoder*, the Supreme Court adjudicated a clash between Wisconsin's compulsory schooling law and the religious beliefs of a local community of Old Order Amish, for whom it was an article of faith that formal education should end with the eighth grade.[23] Notably, the Wisconsin compulsory schooling law at issue permitted alternatives to public school, but like the New York Education Law, required alternative instruction to be "substantially equivalent to instruction given to children of like ages in the public or private schools where such children reside."[24]

The court found for the Old Order Amish. It acknowledged the state interest in regulating the schooling of its population but concluded that the combination of free exercise and the liberty interest of parents in directing the education of their children trump that interest in this case.[25]

Yoder is obviously directly relevant to the yeshiva controversy. If the due process plus free exercise rights of the Amish permitted them to reject formal schooling altogether, a fortiori it should allow a religious group motivated by a religious commitment to establish private schools that teach no secular studies.

However, efforts by religious groups other than the Amish to claim the *Yoder* exception, which are made rarely, generally fail.[26] Both the low rate of claims and the low rate of success are likely due to the fact that *Yoder* does not establish a blanket religious exemption to compulsory schooling. *Yoder* heavily cabined its holding, making it heavily dependent upon the particular claims of the Amish faith and the particular sociology of the Amish community. Three ways in which the Amish differ from the Haredim push hard against the applicability of *Yoder* to the yeshiva controversy.

First, *Yoder* emphasizes that its ruling is narrow. The Amish accepted formal schooling through the eighth grade; they sought to withdraw their children only from an "additional one or two years of formal high school." [27] Moreover, they intended to replace high school with a "long-established program of informal vocational education."[28]

Justice White in his concurrence notes that for him this fact was dispositive. The parents in *Yoder* did not claim that "their religion forbade their children from attending any school at any time and from complying in any way with the educational standards set by the State."[29] White was prepared to permit the religious exemption only because "Amish children are permitted to acquire the basic tools of literacy to survive in modern society by attending grades one through eight."[30] This made the requested "deviation from the State's compulsory education law . . . relatively slight."[31]

Yoder therefore permits religious exemptions only from compulsory high school and is generally read to imply strongly that there is no religious exemption from compulsory education for younger children.

The yeshiva case, of course, involves small children in the early grades. Moreover, the accusations that led to heightened regulation of the yeshivas included claims that students were *not* "permitted to acquire the basic tools of literacy to survive in modern society by attending grades one through eight."

Second, *Yoder*'s exemption rests in part on evidence that the Amish abjuration of formal secondary schooling had no "potential for significant social burden."[32] The *Yoder* court was enamored of Amish self-sufficiency: "The Amish community has been a highly successful social unit within our society, even if apart from the conventional 'mainstream.' Its members are productive and very law-abiding members of society; they reject public welfare in any of its usual modern forms."[33]

Indeed, the court went on, "the record in this case establishes without contradiction that the Green County Amish had never been known to commit crimes, that none had been known to receive public assistance, and that none was unemployed."[34] The religious exemption seems to depend, therefore, on a demonstration that it would not feed dependence, criminality, or idleness.

No data of which I am aware assess criminality among Haredim. However, it is widely observed that unemployment and dependence upon public welfare are endemic in Haredi communities. According to a Pew Center report, nearly 40 percent of Haredi individuals in the United States have a high school diploma or less. Forty-three percent of Haredi households, many of them large families, earn less than $50,000 annually.[35] A study done by the United Jewish Appeal-Federation of New York found that 45 percent of Hasidic households in New York City are poor, while another 18 percent are near poor.[36] Public welfare is a quotidian source of support for Haredi families.[37]

This aspect of *Yoder* has been controversial. Judges today would likely hesitate to discriminate among religious groups based upon their poverty or the rates at which they claim public benefits.[38] Nevertheless, judicial openness to applying *Yoder* might be affected by a record that links Haredi educational practice to welfare dependence.

A third issue, raised in *Yoder*, is that a religious exemption ill serves children who might desire, in the present or the future, to diverge from their parents' religious lifestyle. The majority in *Yoder* held this objection to be irrelevant, both because no children in this position were before it and because parents, not children themselves, make educational decisions.[39] But Justice White raised this issue,[40] and Justice Douglas dissented in part because of it. Douglas explains:

> While the parents, absent dissent, normally speak for the entire family, the education of the child is a matter on which the child will often have decided

views. He may want to be a pianist or an astronaut or an oceanographer. To do so he will have to break from the Amish tradition.

It is the future of the student, not the future of the parents, that is imperiled by today's decision. If a parent keeps his child out of school beyond the grade school, then the child will be forever barred from entry into the new and amazing world of diversity that we have today. The child may decide that that is the preferred course, or he may rebel. It is the student's judgment, not his parents,' that is essential if we are to give full meaning to what we have said about the Bill of Rights and of the right of students to be masters of their own destiny. If he is harnessed to the Amish way of life by those in authority over him, and if his education is truncated, his entire life may be stunted and deformed.[41]

A footnote to this passage cites evidence that substantial numbers of Amish children do in fact leave the community.[42]

Douglas is describing, with almost eerie precision, the complaints of the yeshiva students that catalyzed the changes in New York educational regulation. Writing in the *New York Times*, Shulem Deen, born three years after *Yoder*, lamented a yeshiva education that offered him "not a word about history, geography, science, literature, art or most other [secular] subjects," and only "rudimentary instruction in English and arithmetic."

As an adult, graduated from the yeshiva with "no marketable skills," he reports being beset by "both shame and anger"—and that he is able only partially to compensate for the educational handicaps imposed in his youth.[43] And Deen is no singularity; Haredi children, like Amish children, routinely leave the community as adults.[44]

Justice Douglas, if confronted with a Shulem Deen, clearly would not offer Haredim a religious exemption pursuant to *Yoder.* Justice White wouldn't either.[45] And there is substantial room to doubt whether other judges and justices might be moved to agree, if faced with students who were not theoretical future astronauts or oceanographers, but actual living persons unable to read and write rudimentary English.

These three factors together—that the neglect of secular studies (allegedly) characterizes yeshivas at all ages and grades, that yeshiva graduates frequently depend upon public welfare, and that those graduates who break with the community argue that their education left them incompetent to build their lives as they now wish—strongly suggest that, notwithstanding *Yoder*, Haredi communities and families would *not* be found to have a free exercise right to be exempted from all aspects of compulsory schooling in secular subjects.

LIMITATIONS ON STATE REGULATION

We have established that the state can constitutionally specify that all private schools provide instruction in core subjects like English, mathematics, science, civics, and health at levels consistent with progress from grade to grade as understood in the public system. We have also established that yeshivas are not entitled to a blanket religious exemption.

Therefore, the more maximalist version of the position that might be taken by the yeshivas, that states must permit secular studies programs that are de minimis, is untenable. Even if one demurs to the claim that Haredi children bear a religious duty to engage in religious study at every possible moment,[46] baseline curricular claims of the state trump any such duty.

This does not imply, however, that a state can demand anything it chooses of a private school. In particular, it does not imply that a state can demand what New York State demands, which is that private schools, whether religious or secular, must provide a program of secular study "substantially equivalent" to that required of public schools. The constitutionality of this requirement depends upon what "substantial equivalence" is understood to mean and how the requirement is implemented.[47]

The most fundamental limitation is that the state cannot so thoroughly commandeer a private school that it is unable to further its peculiar mission, and is essentially forced to function as a public school would.[48] For this reason, the Ohio Supreme Court set aside in 1976 a regime that required private schools proportionally to devote most of the school day, however long, to particular subjects. Such a rule, the court reasoned, prevents the private school from engaging in activities central to its mission.[49]

The state, though able to require the teaching of any of a list of secular subjects, is still barred from requiring too many. This is an issue regarding quantity, not content.

If "substantial equivalence" requires too much, therefore, the requirement might be unconstitutional. One might, therefore, allege that the list of "twelve common school branches" that private schools must teach middle schoolers under the New York Education Law is unconstitutionally comprehensive. Because commandeering is a matter of degree, it is unclear whether this allegation would succeed. The section's shorter list of requirements[50] for high schools, however, likely falls well short of commandeering.

With respect to all students, moreover, the state clearly has the constitutional power to require some substantial amount of secular instruction. Were the yeshivas to prevail with a commandeering-focused argument, they would still be required to institute substantial secular curricula. This would involve no risk of forcing them de facto to behave as public schools.

No one familiar with Modern Orthodox day schools, in particular, would say that they effectively have become public schools, or lost the ability to serve their particularistic mission—notwithstanding that they not only meet but exceed New York's requirements regarding secular study. To be sure, the Haredim claim that *their* particularistic mission cannot be fulfilled simultaneously with New York's requirements. But the state need not give private schools the ability to fulfill their mission, only the ability to advance it.

The most difficult and in many ways most interesting question is whether the state can prescribe the *means* as well as subjects of education. The state can require that religious schools teach particular things. Can it also require that they teach them in a particular *way*?[51] Private schools have fought such "programmatic" requirements,[52] including among others demands that students be taught secular subjects only by accredited teachers[53] and that they take certain tests.[54] Several of these sorts of demands are among those made by New York State that have most upset the yeshivas and their allies among schools in the private-education sector.[55]

In *Yoder*, the court justifies its grant of the religious exemption partly by quoting with approval an expert who testifies that informal Amish schooling is effective. This suggests that to the extent that methods requirements simply reflect a state choice about the best pedagogical way to get to some permissible end, private schools that can achieve the required goal in another way should be allowed to do so. Therefore, to take an easy example, the state may not require that schools be open on particular days that conflict with religious observance; students can learn just as well on other days.

Content and methods, however, are not a discrete binary. For example, some advocates of the yeshivas have argued that an exclusively religious curriculum, focused upon Talmud study, is a method that itself furthers secular educational goals to the extent that the state cannot demand more.[56]

These advocates argue with great conviction that Talmud study hones critical thinking and analytical skills. They also attest (accurately) that the Talmud records decisions and disputes that depend upon mathematical calculation, scientific fact, political theory, and literary analysis.[57] The claim appears to be that Talmud study is at least a good a method of educating children, i.e., sharpening their minds, as secular study, and the state therefore must accommodate the yeshivas' methodological choice.

This argument must be rejected as a failed effort to conflate content and method. One might reasonably demur to claims about critical thinking and analysis, but no subset of Talmudic content remotely approaches equivalence to *systematic* instruction in the subjects listed by the New York Code. And—obviously—classical Jewish sources are entirely silent with respect to the English language, modern chemistry, physics and biology, American history, and American civics and government.

Knowledge in these areas is in itself a substantive state interest. The state surely can demand that methods unable to advance that interest not be used.

Similarly, the New York statutes require English to be the language of instruction for those courses the code requires.[58] Is requiring that students be taught secular subjects in English (as opposed to being taught English, a different matter) a substantive educational demand, or is it methodological?

Farrington, noted above, seems to have held the latter when it invalidated a statute prohibiting all instruction in a foreign language.[59] So long as private schools teach English and use English as the language of instruction for part of the curriculum, it might be unconstitutional to forbid them from teaching mathematics or science in a different language. But *Farrington* might not extend to requirements that a *portion* of instruction be in English.

Finally, consider requirements regarding how much time must be devoted to instruction. New York has proposed rules for private schools that measure compliance by "units of study," i.e., minimum number of hours of classroom teaching each year in each required subject.[60] Of all of the requirements that New York imposes, this demand is the most fundamentally objectionable to the yeshivas, who are jealous of every hour devoted to secular knowledge.

Are input requirements for numbers of hours in the classroom substantive, and therefore constitutional? Or is teaching for a particular amount of time just a contingent method, so that if a private school can achieve the learning *outputs* that the state desires, the state must permit it to do so regardless of how few hours are spent in the classroom?

This question seems to me quite difficult. It is hard to see how the number of hours a student spends in class has independent educational value apart from whatever he learns while sitting there. Entirely separate from any religious dispute, and motivated in no small part by the rise of online education, newly empowered voices in American education advocate *competency-based education (CBE)*. CBE posits that what should be required are outputs, i.e., competency in various subjects and skills, rather than inputs, i.e., number of hours of study. Flexibility in terms of curriculum and pace allows individual students to progress based on achievement rather than the amount of time spent learning the subject.

New Hampshire, Michigan, and Ohio have all incorporated competency-based alternative paths for students.[61] In several states, including New York, curriculum documents are written to require both outputs and inputs.[62] And CBE is already in use in some New York public schools.[63] This seems to imply that hours of instruction are programmatic requirements that should bend before the Establishment Clause. However, abrogating input regulations in favor of requirements exclusively for outputs could facilitate wholesale evasion of substantive regulation on the part of private schools. The above discussion of claims that Talmud study can substitute for secular teaching suggests how the evasion might occur.

One response is to suggest that private schools must be able to plausibly demonstrate to regulators, or demonstrate prima facie, that their methods are as likely as the standard credit-hour method to achieve the state's goals. But such a response comes up against the fact that hours of instruction themselves have never been shown systematically to generate desired outputs.[64] Indeed, many public schools that use standard inputs routinely fail to achieve outcome goals; it is not shockingly uncommon for them to fail spectacularly. [65]

Can yeshivas be required to adopt educational practices that not only frustrate their religious objectives (maximizing time for religious study) but cannot be shown to be necessary or even effective at securing the objectives of the state? This seems like an unreasonable requirement that does not further the state's duty to educate. But if it is forbidden, then the state might be powerless to block the all-Talmud pedagogy that has been suggested.

I think that a policy of holding private schools to a more demanding standard regarding CBE or other innovative pedagogies to a higher standard than public schools can be justified, for three reasons. First, given the room that some pedagogies (like CBE) leave for wholesale evasion of substantive requirements, the Supreme Court cases discussed above that endorse substantive regulation imply that requirements to ensure monitoring and compliance are also constitutional. The cases include, for example, teachers' "moral character" and patriotic "dispositions" among the inputs that states may constitutionally require. [66]

Second, public schools are subject to the authority of both public servants in their operation and voters in their governance. These institutions protect public school students from wholesale noncompliance, requiring a different regulatory approach than private schools.

Third, there is no constitutional requirement of equivalent treatment or "fairness" across public and private schools. As long as regulations are lawful, they do not become unconstitutional if they fall more heavily on some schools than others.

In short, the Constitution leaves some room for pushback against particular forms of expansive regulation of religious private schools. But those possibilities are fairly limited. The fundamental principle is that the state has the constitutional authority to demand fairly large commitments of time and resources to secular subjects on the part of private schools, including religious ones like the yeshivas. If the yeshivas are in fact teaching secular studies only de minimis—an allegation that, again, is unproven and contested—the state can force parents to send their children elsewhere.

As with any constitutional analysis, it must be emphasized that what governments constitutionally *may* do is very different from what they *must* do. As a matter of sound policy, the state might choose to be more or less aggressive with private schools than it was in the past, and more or less laissez-faire than it now proposes to be.

There are numerous arguments for and against these positions. Those arguments are critically important—but the U.S. Constitution is agnostic as to them. With regard to mandating secular content and curricula in private, religious schools, the Constitution authorizes states to take a broad range of regulatory approaches.

NOTES

1. N.Y. Educ. Law § 3204 (McKinney 2018). Most other states similarly require certain courses to be taught by private schools, although the substance and timing of those courses vary greatly. The most common requirements are English and some form of American history or government. The states generally require that the courses be taught by a certain grade, or during a certain period of years. U.S. Department of Education, Office of Innovation and Improvement, State Regulation of Private Schools (2009), www.ed.gov/admins/comm/choice/regprivschl/index.html (providing a fifty-state survey of public regulation of private schools); EdChoice, "Private Schools and School Choice Programs Are Regulated, Too," 2019, https://www.edchoice.org/school-choice/regulations/ (visited May 8, 2019).

2. E.g., Joseph Newfield, "Leaving the Community" (letter to the editor), *New Yorker*, May 27, 2019, at 3 ("I was raised . . . in New York City, within the Chabad-Lubavitch movement. Although the Chabad community may seem like a relatively modern Hasidic Jewish sect that is integrated into American society, this perception is far from the truth. The school that my brothers and I attended did not teach the English-language alphabet; we studied the Bible, the Talmud, and Jewish law in Yiddish instead. We also weren't taught any math or science, lest our impressionable minds be polluted by secular knowledge.").

3. The State Education Department informed a New York court that its own investigation "suggested the possibility" that in at least some yeshivas "secular instruction was being treated as optional, not mandatory, and that basic instruction was lacking." Respondents' Memorandum of Law at 9, Parents for Educ. and Religious Liberty in Sch. v. Rosa, No. 901354-19 (N.Y. Sup. Ct. April 17, 2019).

4. Educational powers and duties are explicit in all state constitutions. In federal constitutional law, education is one of the core elements of the "police power," sometimes called "general jurisdiction," defined as those aspects of state sovereignty untouched by the federal constitution. Every state constitution makes this explicit. Although education is surprisingly minimal in American constitutional theorizing, thinkers since antiquity have understood the education of the young to be a paramount function of any state. See Amy Gutmann, *Democratic Education*, rev. ed. (Princeton: Princeton University Press, 1999), 42 ("A Democratic State is therefore committed to allocating educational authority in such a way as to provide its members with an education adequate to participating in democratic politics, to choosing among [a limited range of] good lives, and to sharing in the several subcommunities, such as families, that impart identity to the lives of its citizens.").

5. Eric A. DeGroff, "State Regulation of Nonpublic Schools: Does the Tie Still Bind?," *Brigham Young University Education and Law Journal* 363 (2003): 392. The 1920s private-school cases were decided at a time when the court treated the right freely to contract as an aspect of the liberty guaranteed by the Due Process Clause. The cases therefore focus on the rights of private schools, qua institutions, to conduct their business as they see fit. E.g., Pierce v. Society of Sisters, 268 U.S. 510, 536 (1925) (the Fourteenth Amendment protects private schools from "arbitrary, unreasonable, and unlawful interference with their patrons and the consequent destruction of their business and property"). This contract-focused approach, epitomized by the case of Lochner v. New York, 198 U.S. 45 (1905), was repudiated by the court during the New Deal. See West Coast Hotel Co. v. Parrish, 300 U.S. 379 (1937).The private school cases, however, are universally regarded still as good law. Their principles have been reconceptualized as rules that protect the liberty of parents to direct the education of their children. See Wisconsin v. Yoder, 406 U.S. 205, 233 (1972). This has been fairly straightforward to do, given repeated language in the cases, discussed below, that emphasizes that the state does not have the power to "standardize" children.

6. 268 U.S. 510 (1925).

7. Ibid., 530, 534–35.

8. Ibid., 535.

9. 262 U.S. 390, 397 (1923).

10. 273 U.S. 284, 291 (1927).

11. Ibid., 294.

12. Ibid., 298; accord *Meyer*, 262 U.S., 401 (statute at issue interferes "with the power of parents to control the education of their own").

13. *Meyer*, 262 U.S., 402. See also ibid., 401, "That the state may do much, go very far, indeed, in order to improve the quality of its citizens, physically, mentally and morally, is clear; but the individual has certain fundamental rights which must be respected."

14. *Pierce*, 268 U.S., 534.

15. *Meyer*, 262 U.S., 401.

16. Runyon v. McCrary, 427 U.S. 160, 178 (1976).

17. See infra note and accompanying text.

18. See Derek W. Black, "The Constitutional Compromise to Guarantee Education," *Stanford Law Review* 70, no. 3 (March 2018): 735, 795. "Given the opportunity, the Reconstruction-era state conventions saw education as essential to the operation of their own republican forms of government at the state and local levels. Even to this day, state supreme courts regularly justify aggressive interpretations of education clauses by citing the Framers' original democratic intent: ensuring that citizens can discharge their duties at the ballot box and on juries." For examples, see Connecticut Coal. for Justice in Educ. Funding, Inc. v. Rell, 990 A.2d 206, 212 (Conn. 2010) (plurality opinion); Mack v. Bd. of Educ. of Pub. Sch. of Robeson Cty., 748 S.E.2d 774 (N.C. 2013) ("[T]he right to a sound basic education includes . . . sufficient fundamental knowledge of geography, history, and basic economic and political systems to enable the student to make informed choices with regard to issues that affect the student personally or affect the student's community, state, and nation.") (internal quotations omitted); Aristy-Farer v. State, 81 N.E.3d 360, 363 (N.Y. 2017) ("[O]ur State Constitution requires the State to offer all children the opportunity of a sound basic education. Such an education should consist of the basic literacy, calculating, and verbal skills necessary to enable children to eventually function productively as civic participants capable of voting and serving on a jury.") (internal quotations omitted) (quoting Campaign for Fiscal Equity, Inc. v. State, 655 N.E.2d 661, 666 [N.Y. 1995]).

19. See Campaign for Fiscal Equity, Inc. v. State, 655 N.E.2d 661, 666 (N.Y. 1995). "Children are also entitled to minimally adequate teaching of reasonably up-to-date basic curricula such as reading, writing, mathematics, science, and social studies, by sufficient personnel adequately trained to teach those subject areas." The court of appeals treats this as a core police power.

20. Meyer v. Nebraska, 262 U.S. 390, 402 (1923). "The power of the State to compel attendance at some school and to make reasonable regulations for all schools, including a requirement that they shall give instructions in English, is not questioned."

21. See *Pierce*, 268 U.S. at 535; see also *Whisner*, 351 N.E.2d at 768 (Ohio 1976), invalidating state education standards that would "effectively eradicate the distinction between public and non-public education."

22. Wisconsin v. Yoder, 406 U.S. 205 (1972).

23. Ibid.

24. Ibid., 237 (quoting Wis. Stat. § 118.15[4] [1969]).

25. Ibid., 233–35.

26. E.g., State v. Faith Baptist Church of Louisville, 301 N.W.2d 571, 573, 579-80 (Neb. 1981) (upholding Nebraska school regulations that required certain subjects be taught, limited operating hours, and set standards for teacher qualification against a parochial school's Free Exercise challenge because "[t]he requirements as to curriculum as imposed by the state board appear to be very minimal in nature. . . . The refusal of the defendants to comply with the compulsory education laws of the State of Nebraska as applied in this case is an arbitrary and unreasonable attempt to thwart the legitimate, reasonable, and compelling interests of the State in carrying out its educational obligations, under a claim of religious freedom.").

27. *Yoder*, 406 U.S., 222.

28. Ibid.

29. Ibid., 238 (White, J., concurring).

30. Ibid.

31. Ibid.

32. Ibid., 234 (majority opinion).

33. Ibid., 222.

34. Ibid., 222 n.11.

35. Pew Research Center, "A Portrait of American Orthodox Jews," Religion and Public Life, August 26, 2015, 14–15, https://www.pewforum.org/2015/08/26/a-portrait-of-american-orthodox-jews/.

36. Jacob B. Ukeles, Steven M. Cohen, and Ron Miller, "Jewish Community Study of New York: 2011: Special Report on Poverty." UJA-Federation of New York, June 2013, 54–56, https://www.ujafedny.org/assets/785329.

37. Quantitative data on unemployment and welfare do not categorize populations by religion. However, in Borough Park, 4.9 percent of households receive cash public assistance, 36.1 percent of households have received Supplemental Nutrition Assistance Program (SNAP) in the last 12 months, and 67.5 percent of the noninstitutionalized civilian population have health insurance through public coverage. In Williamsburg, 6.3 percent of households receive cash public assistance, 51.1 percent of households have received SNAP in the last 12 months, and 77.6 percent of the noninstitutionalized civilian population have health insurance through public coverage. The New York City averages for those same programs are 4.3 percent, 20.2 percent, and 42.0 percent respectively. See NYC Planning Population FactFinder, https://popfactfinder.planning.nyc.gov/#12.25/40.724/-73.9868 (last visited July 16, 2019).

38. *Yoder*, 406 U.S. at 246 (Douglas, J., dissenting in part) ("I think the emphasis of the Court on the 'law and order' record of this Amish group of people is quite irrelevant. A religion is a religion irrespective of what the misdemeanor or felony records of its members might be.").

39. Ibid., 224, 231–32 (majority opinion).

40. White echoes Douglas's language, noting with concern that some Amish children "may wish to become nuclear physicists, ballet dancers, computer programmers, or historians," but would not have been prepared for such occupations. Ibid., 240 (White, J., concurring). But White ultimately joins the majority. Ibid., 241.

41. Ibid., 244–46 (Douglas, J., dissenting in part) (internal footnotes omitted).

42. Ibid., 245 n.2.

43. See Shulem Deen, "Why Is New York City Condoning Illiteracy?," *New York Times*, April 4, 2018, 60, https://www.nytimes.com/2018/04/04/opinion/yeshivas-literacy-new-york.html; *accord supra* note 2; see also Elizabeth Llorente, "Hasidic 'Defectors' Find Challenges, Isolation in Pursuing a New Life," *Fox News*, June 14, 2018, https://www.foxnews.com/us/hasidic-defectors-find-challenges-isolation-in-pursuing-a-new-life.

44. See Pew Research Center, "A Portrait of American Orthodox Jews," 49 ("Though Orthodox Jews today make up 10% of the net Jewish population and 12% of current Jews by religion, larger numbers [14% of all Jews and 17% of Jews by religion] say they were raised as Orthodox. This reflects a high rate of attrition from Orthodox Judaism, especially among older cohorts. Among those 65 and older who were raised as Orthodox Jews, just 22% are still Orthodox Jews by religion. And among those ages 50–64 who were raised Orthodox, just 41% are still Orthodox Jews by religion. In stark contrast, 83% of Jewish adults under 30 who were raised Orthodox are still Orthodox.").

45. White was more sympathetic to such children than the rest of the majority, echoing Douglas in noting that some Amish children "may wish to become nuclear physicists, ballet dancers, computer programmers, or historians," occupations for which high school is a necessity. *Yoder*, 240 (White, J., concurring). But White ultimately joins the *Yoder* majority. Ibid., 241.

46. It is unintelligible to interpret "every possible moment" literally. See Mishna Peah 1:1 (the obligation of study "has no fixed quantity," i.e., can expand to fill however much time is allotted to it).

47. Obviously, the state cannot require private schools *not* to teach things that are not taught in public school—like religion. But no one takes "substantial equivalence" to mean "no significant content in addition to." Such a construction, though semantically plausible, is both perverse and unconstitutional.

48. The state also may not be motivated by religious animus. Such animus does not appear in New York and has not been alleged. In federal law, the constitutional baseline rule is that regulations that do not particularly target religion and are not motivated by religious animus do

not violate the First Amendment even if they burden particular religious practices. *See* Employment Div., Dep't of Human Res. of Oregon v. Smith, 494 U.S. 872, 878, 882 (1990). But *Smith* specifically excepts religious schools from its scope, because it is a "hybrid" of two constitutional rights, not just free exercise but also the liberty to educate one's children. *See* ibid., 881 ("The only decisions in which we have held that the First Amendment bars application of a neutral, generally applicable law to religiously motivated action have involved not the Free Exercise Clause alone, but the Free Exercise Clause in conjunction with other constitutional protections, such as freedom of speech . . . or the right of parents . . . to direct the education of their children.") (internal citations omitted). This approach respects the absolute centrality of education in many religious worldviews, that of the Haredim certainly among them.

49. See Ohio v. Whisner, 351 N.E.2d 750, 765 (Ohio 1976) ("We think that [the regulation] 'unduly burdens the free exercise of religion' and interferes 'with the rights of conscience,' by requiring a set amount of time [on a percentage basis] to be devoted to subjects which, by their very nature, may not easily lend themselves to the teaching of religious principles.").

50. "[A]t least the English language and its use, in civics, hygiene, physical training, and American history including the principles of government." N.Y. Educ. Law § 3204(3)(2) (McKinney 2019).

51. See DeGroff, "State Regulation of Nonpublic Schools," 392. Although the federal constitution permits states to require private schools to instruct students in particular subjects, "the state may not dictate the manner in which required subjects are taught."

52. See E. Vance Randall, "Private Schools and State Regulation," *The Urban Lawyer* 24, no. 2 (1992): 341, 370 ("Private school regulations are . . . primarily programmatic in character and focus on the ingredients that conventional wisdom says must be present to ensure quality education—items such as instructional time, teacher certification, teacher/pupil ratio, class size, curriculum, adequate physical facilities, etc.").

53. DeGroff, "State Regulation of Nonpublic Schools," 387 ("As to the legality of teacher certification requirements [with respect to teachers of secular subjects], the United States Supreme Court has never forbidden such a practice. Among the state courts, teacher certification requirements have been upheld, although the supreme courts of Ohio, Kentucky and Vermont have overturned what they considered overly pervasive regulatory schemes that happened to include such requirements."). See generally Fellowship Baptist Church v. Benton, 815 F.2d 485 (8th Cir. 1987); People v. Bennett, 501 N.W.2d 106 (Mich. 1993); State v. Anderson, 427 N.W.2d 316, 317 (N.D. 1988).

54. DeGroff, "State Regulation of Nonpublic Schools," 383 n.92 ("States that require private schools to report the results of student testing include Alaska, Idaho, Indiana, Kansas, Minnesota, Mississippi, Nebraska, New Mexico, New York, North Carolina, North Dakota, Ohio, Pennsylvania, South Dakota, Tennessee, Vermont, West Virginia and Wyoming."). See also Ohio Ass'n of Indep. Sch. v. Goff, 92 F.3d 419, 424 (6th Cir. 1996) ("In light of the state's interest in education, a reasonable basis exists for utilizing a testing requirement to ensure that students from both public and private schools meet certain basic standards.").

55. See N.Y. Department of Education, Local School Authority Review (2018) (requiring that "English shall be the language of instruction for common branch subjects . . . Instruction may be given only by a competent teacher."); 41 N.Y. Reg. 2 (proposed July 3, 2019) ("[T]he Commissioner, when he/she is responsible for making the [substantial equivalency] determination, must consider the following criteria: Instruction given only by a competent teacher . . . English is the language of instruction for common branch subjects.").

56. See Affidavit of Israel M. Kirzner at 9, Parents for Educ. and Religious Liberty in Sch. v. Rosa, No. 901354-19 (N.Y. Sup. Ct. Apr. 17, 2019) ("Rabbi Hutner molded the educational program at [Mesivta Yeshiva Rabbi Chaim Berlin] to ensure that his students were fully equipped to achieve the goals he envisioned for them. Given the rigorous training in consistent logic and intellectual honesty required to meet MYRCB's Talmudic standards, its graduates were (and are) in fact better-equipped than students of secular institutions, whose background lacked that training."); Affidavit of Aaron D. Twerski at 9, Parents for Educ. and Religious Liberty in Sch. v. Rosa, No. 901354-19 (N.Y. Sup. Ct. Apr. 17, 2019) ("[A] yeshiva education provides students with a critical thinking and analytical skills that far surpass those obtained by students at traditional schools."); Menachem Wecker, "New York State Cracks Down on Jewish Schools," *Education Next* 19, no.

40 (Fall 2019), https://www.educationnext.org/new-york-state-cracks-down-jewish-schools-senator-simcha-felder-rabbi-chaim-dovid-zwiebel-joseph-hodges-choate ("Rabbis teaching Talmud don't quite ask the same sorts of questions that university professors do, but they often cold-call upon their young students to probe sophisticated questions about ancient and medieval texts. And like law professors, they frequently ask follow-up questions that require students to articulate arguments in a way that demonstrates their grasp of essential points.").

57. Cf. Mishna Avot 5:22 ("Everything is [included] in" Torah study).

58. "In the teaching of the subjects of instruction prescribed by this section, English shall be the language of instruction." N.Y. Educ. Law § 3204(2)(i) (McKinney 2019); *accord* 41 N.Y. Reg. 2 (proposed July 3, 2019).

59. See *supra* notes 10–11 and accompanying text.

60. "Whether the instructional program in the nonpublic school incorporates instruction in the following subjects . . . mathematics (two units of study); English language arts (two units of study); social studies (two units of study); science (two units of study)." 41 N.Y. Reg. 2 (proposed July 3, 2019). These units, which professional educators sometimes call "Carnegie units," have been used by American schools for many years to quantify instruction in terms of hours in the classroom. Carnegie Foundation for the Advancement of Teaching, "FAQs," Carnegie Foundation, https://www.carnegiefoundation.org/faqs/ (last visited June 6, 2019) ("The unit was developed in 1906 as a measure of the amount of time a student has studied a subject. For example, a total of 120 hours in one subject—meeting 4 or 5 times a week for 40 to 60 minutes, for 36 to 40 weeks each year—earns the student one 'unit' of high school credit."). The unit became widespread in the early twentieth century when Andrew Carnegie established a ten-million-dollar pension fund for college teachers. To be eligible for the fund, colleges were required to use the "Carnegie Unit" plan for admission. Jessica M. Shedd, "The History of the Student Credit Hour," *New Directions for Higher Education* 122 (Summer 2003): 5, 7.

61. U.S. Department of Education, Competency-Based Learning or Personalized Learning, https://www.ed.gov/oii-news/competency-based-learning-or-personalized-learning (last visited July 18, 2019).

62. See, e.g., N.Y. Comp. Codes R. & Regs. tit. 8, § 100.4 ("During grades 5 and 6, all students shall receive instruction that is designed to *facilitate their attainment of the State intermediate learning standards* in the seven general curriculum areas: mathematics, . . . English language arts, . . . social studies, . . . languages other than English, . . . the arts, . . . career development and occupational studies[,] . . . and health education.") (emphasis added).

63. Kyle Spencer, "A New Kind of Classroom: No Grades, No Failing, No Hurry," *New York Times*, August 11, 2017, https://www.nytimes.com/2017/08/11/nyregion/mastery-based-learning-no-grades.html.

64. Randall, "Private Schools and State Regulation," 370 ("Empirical research, however, reveals that there is little if any correlation, let alone causal connection, between these specific types of educational 'inputs' and academic achievement or other educational outcomes."); Shedd, "The History of the Student Credit Hour," 11.

65. Cf. Zelman v. Simmons-Harris, 536 U.S. 639, 681, (2002) (Thomas, J., concurring) ("Of Cleveland eighth graders taking the 1999 Ohio proficiency test, 95 percent in Catholic schools passed the reading test, whereas only 57 percent in public schools passed. And 75 percent of Catholic school students passed the math proficiency test, compared to only 22 percent of public school students.").

66. Pierce v. Society of Sisters, 268 U.S. 510, 534 (1925).

Chapter Five

The Yeshiva Case

A Legal Path Forward

Howard Slugh and Devorah Goldman[1]

In 1892, the Volozhin yeshiva—widely known as "the mother of all yeshivas"—was forced to shut down. For nearly a hundred years, it had flourished as a center of Torah learning throughout the Lithuanian Jewish world, influencing communities far beyond its namesake Russian town. Closing the school, though, took a matter of weeks: on December 22, 1891, the Russian minister of education published a set of regulations demanding that the school transform its curriculum to conform to government standards. Volozhin's leadership refused, and the yeshiva was shuttered in late January.

This was not the end of Volozhin. Community leaders fought for the right to study and teach as they saw fit, and the school was reopened on a limited basis years later and remained active in some capacity until World War II. Its continued impact on Jewish communities today is a testament not only to the brilliance of Volozhin's individual scholars, but to the seriousness with which observant Jews engage in a particular tradition of learning—one that many believe is worth sacrificing for.

In recent years, parochial schools run by "Haredi Orthodox Jews," a term that encompasses a range of observant Jewish groups including certain Hasidic sects, have also faced mandates requiring them to better comply with specific secular education standards. Since 2015, New York authorities on both the state and city levels have attempted to exert greater control over the curricula of yeshivas in a manner reminiscent of the Russian government's behavior at the turn of the nineteenth century. To understand how best to defend these yeshivas, it is important to understand the particulars of the conflict in question, as well as key court cases involving related issues.

As we will see, there are several legal doctrines that the yeshivas can use to shield themselves against government intrusion, each of which has its own strengths and weaknesses. Given the flaws in each form of defense, we advocate for two legal changes that would provide yeshivas and other parochial schools with more robust and dependable protection.

SMITH SIGNIFICANTLY NARROWS THE SCOPE OF THE FREE EXERCISE CLAUSE

As described in the introduction to this book, the yeshivas in question have successfully defended themselves on procedural grounds so far. Nevertheless, arguments based on religious liberty might play a greater role in future challenges.

In this and other cases in which religious freedom appears to be at risk, some legal experts and the public may invoke the First Amendment's Free Exercise Clause, which prevents Congress from making laws "prohibiting the free exercise" of religion. While originally understood as only restricting the federal government, the Supreme Court held in 1940 that the Fourteenth Amendment extended the First Amendment's prohibition to state and local governments. Understanding key cases dealing with free exercise will be important in understanding the yeshiva controversy.

A useful though unhappy place to begin is *Employment Division v. Smith*, a 1990 Supreme Court case that upended the preexisting Free Exercise jurisprudence and replaced it with a far less protective regime. *Smith* involved a challenge brought by two Native Americans who had been fired from their jobs as drug counselors for ingesting the illegal drug peyote as part of a religious ritual. They were denied federal unemployment benefits because they were judged to have been fired due to their illegal conduct.

The counselors took their case to the courts, arguing that they should not have been denied government benefits because the cause of their dismissal— ingesting peyote for religious purposes—was protected by the Free Exercise Clause. Oregon's Supreme Court agreed, and ruled that the state's drug prohibition must contain an exception for religious use.

The Supreme Court reversed this ruling. In an opinion that stunned many in the legal world, Justice Antonin Scalia concluded that the Free Exercise Clause does not shield religiously motivated actions from "neutral and generally applicable" laws. In other words, unless a law singles out religion for disfavored treatment, simply imposing a burden on a religious practice would not render a nondiscriminatory, general law unconstitutional under the Free Exercise Clause.

This effectively transformed the Free Exercise clause into more of an antidiscrimination provision than a broad protection for religious conduct.

Scalia asserted that those seeking exemptions from generally applicable legal requirements for religious reasons should seek redress in the political arena rather than the courts.

RFRA REJUVENATES RELIGIOUS LIBERTY PROTECTIONS—BUT ONLY FOR FEDERAL CASES

Following *Smith*, many advocates of religious liberty sought to do just that. Civil-rights groups and religious organizations saw the ruling as a significant departure from long-standing judicial protections of free-exercise rights. To ameliorate this, a broad coalition of civil-rights organizations, including the ACLU and the Christian Legal Society, lobbied for a bill that would restore the pre-Smith protections. That bill was the federal Religious Freedom Restoration Act (RFRA), which Congress passed in 1993.

Under RFRA, laws that impose a substantial burden upon religious practices are subject to the "strict scrutiny" test, the most stringent form of judicial review. This means that even a neutral, generally applicable law must be overturned if it burdens religious practice, unless the government can demonstrate that the law is the least restrictive way to further a compelling government interest.

Originally, the federal RFRA applied to federal, state, and local governments. That changed, though, with the 1997 Supreme Court case *City of Boerne v. Flores*. A Catholic archbishop living in Boerne, Texas, sought to expand a church building but was forbidden from doing so because of local historic-preservation rules. The archbishop sued local zoning authorities for violating his rights under RFRA, but the Supreme Court concluded that, due to federalism concerns, the law could apply only to the federal government and could not override the local ordinance.

Since then, twenty-one states have passed state versions of RFRA to provide their citizens protections similar to those offered by the federal RFRA. These laws protect individuals whose religious practices would be burdened by generally applicable laws in their states or localities, and they are particularly important for minority faiths.

Smith poses unique risks to those groups for two reasons: first, little-known or little-understood rituals among minority faiths are more likely to come into conflict with generally applicable laws. For example, the majority is more likely to innocently burden the observance of little-known Jewish holidays like the Ninth of Av than they are to burden the observance of well-known Christian holidays like Christmas. Second, members of minority faiths are less likely to have the political clout to follow Justice Scalia's suggestion and obtain political exemptions on a case-by-case basis.

If the federal RFRA still applied to the states, the New York yeshivas would likely have been able to demonstrate that the state's regulations substantially burdened their religious practice. That would have shifted the burden to New York State to prove that their rules offered the only way to further a compelling government interest. But because the federal RFRA applies only to federal laws, and New York has not passed its own RFRA, its religious citizens are vulnerable.

THE *LUKUMI* EXCEPTION: A POTENTIAL PATH TO VICTORY

Several months before the passage of the federal RFRA, the Supreme Court issued another significant ruling interpreting the Free Exercise Clause, in *Church of Lukumi Babalu Aye v. City of Hialeah*. The case involved Santeria, a Cuban hybrid religion that combines elements of Roman Catholicism with certain traditional African religions, which requires animal sacrifice during various religious rites.

In 1987, members of the Church of Lukumi Babalu Aye, a nonprofit organization established by a Santerian priest, sought to establish a house of worship in Hialeah, Florida. This led to a community uproar and an emergency public session of the city council, during which participants made hostile comments about Santerians. Not long after the meeting, the council released a resolution expressing its "concern that certain religions may propose to engage in practices which are inconsistent with public morals, peace or safety," and specifically declaring its opposition to "the ritual sacrifices of animals."

Three months later, the council unanimously adopted ordinances that prohibited possessing an animal for the purpose of ritual sacrifice. They also banned animal sacrifice within city limits and prohibited animal slaughter outside of areas zoned for slaughterhouses. The rules contained a number of exceptions, such as for kosher slaughter or for euthanasia of stray animals.

In response, members of the church sued the city, alleging a free-exercise violation. On its face, it seemed that this law was constitutionally permissible under *Smith* because it applied to everyone and did not single out the Santeria faith. Nonetheless, the court concluded that the city had failed "to meet the *Smith* standard." It argued that, unlike the broadly applicable peyote law that incidentally infringed on Native American religious practices, the Hialeah ordinances were specifically crafted to target Santerians.

The court cited the overtly antagonistic statements made at the public meeting and remarked upon the ordinances' many exceptions for scientific research, euthanasia, or kosher slaughter that effectively left only Santeria's rituals subject to the prohibitions. The court concluded that, though the statute presented itself as generally applicable, upon closer inspection it was found to target Santerians and was therefore subject to strict scrutiny.

While the court in *Lukumi* claimed to be merely applying *Smith*, a close reading indicates that it departed from *Smith*'s holding, thus creating an exception to the *Smith* standard. In her dissent from the majority ruling in *Smith*, Justice Sandra Day O'Connor maintained that "few States would be so naive as to enact a law directly prohibiting or burdening a religious practice as such."

To O'Connor and others, *Smith* was understood as prohibiting only explicit bans on religious practices. So while a generally applicable law banning circumcision for health reasons could be permissible according to the original understanding of *Smith*, directly banning only Jews from circumcising their children during a religious ritual would not be. Under *Lukumi*, even a superficially neutral ban on circumcision would be unconstitutional if there was evidence that either the lawmaker's intent or the law's enforcement targeted Jews.

Recently, in *Masterpiece Cakeshop v. Colorado Civil Rights Commission*, the court reaffirmed and built upon *Lukumi*. In *Masterpiece*, the court reversed the Colorado Civil Rights Commission's determination that Jack Phillips, a baker, had violated an antidiscrimination law by refusing to create customized cakes for same-sex weddings.

In its 2018 ruling, the court found that the commission's determination was invalid because it had made disparaging comments relating to Phillips and his faith, and because it enforced the law against Phillips while exempting secular bakers. While the law was found to be neutral on its face, its enforcement against Phillips was infected with unconstitutional antireligious animus.

While this is certainly a step in the right direction, it by no means undoes the harm created by *Smith*. First, it is difficult to prove that an explicitly neutral law actually targets religion. In both *Lukumi* and *Masterpiece*, the plaintiffs had remarkably strong evidence demonstrating antireligious motives on the part of their opponents. It is likely that at least some lawmakers or regulators with improper antireligious motives will successfully conceal them in the future. Second, an objectionable law that is nonetheless neutral and generally applicable, like a ban on circumcision that don't target Jewish practices, would still be permitted under any of the cases discussed above.

The lessons to be drawn from these cases are clear: state RFRAs provide important protections for religious liberty, and *Lukumi* provides some protection against laws that demonstrably, even if not explicitly, single out religions. As the yeshiva saga continues to unfold, it is vital to consider both methods of protection.

The yeshivas might be able to make a claim under *Lukumi*, though it will depend on the facts that they can develop regarding the motivations behind the regulations and the manner in which they are enforced. This might be feasible, as the regulations have been used to target religious schools. In other words, it may be possible to demonstrate that regulations based on the amendment are discriminatory because they have been crafted to target religious practices, and are therefore not generally applicable. This is by no means guaranteed, however.

If the yeshivas win on this point, the state would be required to demonstrate that the regulations are necessary to further a compelling government interest.

NEW YORK STATE'S FREE EXERCISE CLAUSE OFFERS LIMITED PROTECTION

The New York State constitution provides a third possible shield that the yeshivas can use to defend themselves against future regulations. The state constitution has its own Free Exercise Clause, which provides additional protection from that offered by the federal Constitution: it proclaims that "free exercise and enjoyment of religious profession and worship, without discrimination of preference, shall forever be allowed in this state to all humankind."

New York does not have to follow *Smith* when interpreting its own constitution and is free to provide greater protection of religious liberty. Unfortunately, this potential defense suffers from its own deficiencies.

Following *Smith*, some state courts adopted interpretations similar to *Smith*, while others rejected that narrow view of religious liberty. New York did not answer this question until 2006, nearly a decade after *Lukumi* was decided and the federal RFRA was passed.

In 2002, New York's legislature passed the Women's Health and Wellness Act, which mandated that health-insurance coverage include women's services. Specifically, any plan that covered prescription drugs was required to cover the cost of contraceptive drugs and devices. The act included a four-part definition of "religious employers" and allowed employers that fell into this category to request an insurance contract that did not cover contraception.

Ten faith-based social-service organizations, including the Catholic Charities of the Diocese of Albany, sued New York State officials, claiming that the act violated the Free Exercise Clauses of both the federal and New York State constitutions. None of the employers suing in *Catholic Charities of the Diocese of Albany v. Serio* met the criteria for the "religious employer" exemption, because they either served or employed many individuals who did not share their faith (the law's four-part definition of "religious employer" entailed that employers primarily serve and primarily employ individuals who shared the employer's faith). The employers were therefore required to pay for contraception, which violated their religious principles. The other alternative suggested to them was to circumvent the law by refusing *all* prescription-drug coverage in their health-insurance plans, but Catholic Charities believed that this would violate their religious obligation to provide employees a just wage. They did not seek to invalidate the law entirely, but simply to be included in the exemption.

In 2006, New York's Court of Appeals, the highest court in the state, held that the law did not violate the groups' free-exercise rights under the federal constitution. It found that the law's requirement was neutral and generally applicable, and so did not violate the federal Constitution's Free Exercise Clause according to *Smith*. Having dispensed with the federal issues, this neatly teed up the question of whether the Court of Appeals would apply *Smith*'s reasoning to its own constitution.

At first, the Court of Appeals seemed to move in a positive direction. It rejected *Smith* as "inflexible" and refused to interpret the New York State Free Exercise Clause that narrowly. The court held that the state Free Exercise Clause would apply to all laws, even those that were neutral and generally applicable. At that point, one might have thought that this meant the state would need to demonstrate that its law was the least burdensome way to further a compelling government interest, as was the case under federal law prior to *Smith*. Unfortunately, that was not the end of the story.

Just as the court held that the state Free Exercise Clause would apply, it held that the clause was not a particularly burdensome obstacle for the legislature to overcome. The court rejected the robust free-exercise protections that existed at the federal level prior to *Smith* or under RFRA. Instead, the court held that it would balance the burden that a law places on a religious adherent against the legislature's interest in passing the law.

To make matters worse, this "balancing" would not occur on a neutral playing field: the court would grant "substantial deference" to the legislature and require that the religious adherent prove the legislature had acted "unreasonably." The deck would be stacked against religious plaintiffs, and the court frankly admitted that such plaintiffs would usually lose.

When applying this test, the court predictably found that the state's interest in fostering equality between the sexes and providing women with better health care outweighed the plaintiffs' interest in following their faith.

New York's constitution, unlike the federal one, would apply to the yeshivas' hypothetical claims. Unfortunately, that means only that a New York court would ask whether the law was "reasonable," while giving "substantial deference" to the legislature. This is still better than the federal Constitution, which, as it has been interpreted by the Supreme Court, offers no protection against genuinely neutral laws. Despite this relative advantage, New York's constitution offers a flimsy defense of religious exercise. In practice, New York courts are no more hospitable to free-exercise claims than federal courts operating under *Smith*.

THE PROMISE AND RISKS OF SUBSTANTIVE DUE PROCESS

Some have suggested that yeshiva advocates invoke the Fourteenth Amendment's Due Process Clause, which requires government officials to follow neutral procedures, including providing notice and a fair hearing before depriving a person of life, liberty, or property. The Supreme Court, though, has sometimes interpreted this clause to protect certain "substantive" rights rather than simple procedural fairness. In practice, this has meant that the court has *created* a set of rights that justices have claimed are essential to life, liberty, and property—sometimes with damaging results.

One such case, *Pierce v. Society of Sisters*, involved a 1922 Oregon referendum that required all school-age children to attend public schools, with limited exceptions. The amended Compulsory Education Act, which was promoted by Protestant groups and even the Ku Klux Klan, was largely seen as targeting Catholics and other religious minorities, many of whom sent their children to religious private schools.

The Society of Sisters, a Catholic organization that ran several schools in Oregon, sued state officials over the law, arguing that it violated the Contracts Clause and the Due Process Clause of the Fourteenth Amendment. Their case was consolidated with a separate challenge brought by the Hill Military Academy, a secular private school. The case made its way to the Supreme Court, which ruled that the law violated the "liberty of parents and guardians to direct the upbringing and education of children under their control."

This case is often invoked as a victory for religious liberty: Stephen Carter of Yale Law School, for example, wrote that "what *Pierce* ultimately represents is the judgment that in order to take religious freedom seriously, we must take the ability of parents to raise their children in their religion seriously." But while the Society of Sisters argued in its bill of complaint that the "pretended law attempts to control the free exercise and enjoyment of religious opinions and to interfere with the rights of conscience," it never explicitly invoked the Free Exercise Clause. At that time, it couldn't have— the clause was not incorporated against the states until 1940.

The Supreme Court declined to rule on religious-liberty grounds, despite the fact that both sides invoked religious liberty in their respective arguments (indeed, the court did not even reference the arguments related to religious liberty).

By articulating a "liberty interest" grounded in the right "of parents and guardians to direct the upbringing and education of children under their control," the Supreme Court's ruling signified a step forward for "substantive due process." While some celebrated the result in this instance, this doctrine gives the court wide latitude to impose its own values or policy preferences.

There are a number of downsides to relying on substantive due process. First, decisions based on that doctrine are notoriously difficult to predict. Judges applying substantive due process effectively answer the question of what they think the law *ought* to be rather than what they think the law actually is. This is not a steady foundation upon which to build a defense of religious schools. Perhaps it should be included as one of many defenses, but it is by no means a sturdy, predictable shield.

Perhaps even more troubling, relying on the sort of substantive due process used in the court's *Pierce* decision can—and has—yielded negative consequences for advocates of religious liberty.

While the immediate results of *Pierce* seem appealing, as the court's ruling preserved the right of parents to send their children to religious private schools, the decision has also been cited in support of abortion rights (such as in *Planned Parenthood v. Casey*), access to contraception (in *Griswold v. Connecticut*), and gay marriage (in *Obergefell v. Hodges*). These changes, which stem at least in part from the same underlying reasoning as the *Pierce* decision, have profoundly affected areas in which religion once played a predominant role in inculcating values.

Beyond the ongoing concrete effects of *Pierce*, it is also objectionable to many who agree with Justice Clarence Thomas that the "the Fourteenth Amendment's Due Process Clause is not a secret repository of substantive guarantees against unfairness." In other words, in the interest of maintaining an intellectually consistent and democratically legitimate jurisprudence, it is best not to rely on the legacy of substantive due process.

It is difficult to determine the likelihood of success the yeshivas would have if they brought a substantive due process claim. Such claims are unpredictable at best, since they lack any concrete standards or textual guideposts. Additionally, given the history of the doctrine, any gains that the yeshivas make by utilizing substantive due process may come back to haunt them.

THE IMPORTANCE OF PASSING A STATE RFRA LAW AND RECONSIDERING *SMITH*

One key lesson to be drawn from the above cases concerns the importance of passing a RFRA law in New York. This would solve many of the issues at play in the ongoing yeshiva skirmishes. RFRA bills have been introduced in the state legislature in the past but have never gotten very far. This is in part because the opponents of the legislation have managed to convince many among the public that such bills are used by the majority to oppress vulnerable minorities.

As we discussed above, this is exactly backward—religious minorities benefit the most from RFRA laws and suffer the most in their absence. Perhaps New York's Jewish citizens can help restore the good reputation that RFRA enjoyed in 1993 by demonstrating how important such laws are to religious minorities who simply want to teach their children in a traditional manner and have no interest in oppressing any other group.

A second important lesson is that supporters of the yeshivas should urge the Supreme Court to reconsider its *Smith* decision. Fortunately, members of the Supreme Court have signaled their openness to doing exactly that. Writing for four justices, Justice Alito recently acknowledged that *Smith* "drastically cut back on the protection provided by the Free Exercise Clause." Alito went on to imply that perhaps it was time to "revisit" *Smith*.

The Supreme Court quickly acted upon Justice Alito's suggestion. It recently agreed to review the case *Fulton v. Philadelphia*, which presents the question of "whether *Employment Division v. Smith* should be revisited." Jewish communal organizations should file amicus briefs explaining how harmful *Smith* has been to minority faiths.

Jewish organizations and individuals have a necessary and powerful role to play in America's ongoing discussions regarding religious liberty. Situations such as the conflict over New York's yeshivas demonstrate how grave the stakes can be. Jewish Americans cannot afford to view religious liberty as a problem for someone else to deal with. If we want to protect our rights, it is imperative that we join in this discussion on the side of religious liberty.

NOTE

1. They are grateful to Julie Borzage for her assistance in preparing research.

Chapter Six

Challenges to Educational Freedom in Europe

Charles L. Glenn

In discussing educational freedom, it is important to make a distinction between instruction and education. The former refers to the teaching of skills and information, the latter to the formation of character and values on the basis of a coherent—and often distinctive—understanding of the requirements of a flourishing life.

Government is generally conceded authority to protect the interests of children by ensuring that they are instructed adequately, whether in schools that it manages directly, in private schools, or by homeschooling. There is room for disagreement about what skills and knowledge are needed for different life trajectories, and whether government has a right to substitute its understanding of appropriate careers for that of parents and youth.

For example, in *Wisconsin v. Jonas Yoder* (1972), the U.S. Supreme Court decided that the Amish had a right to choose an alternative lifestyle. Current controversies in Israel, Britain, and the United States over the scope and adequacy of instruction provided in yeshivas to teenage boys from Orthodox Jewish families illustrate this tension over government-defined instructional standards. As we will see, these assertions of the right of the state to define the knowledge and skills that youth should acquire from their schooling inevitably infringe upon the religious freedom of citizens.

But it is with respect to *education* that controversies arise most frequently. Should the authority of government extend to prescribing the values, character, and worldview that nongovernment schools seek to develop? Is it not the responsibility of parents to nurture the character of their children on the basis of their best judgment and their deep convictions? While rendering lip service to this principle, some Western governments are tempted—claiming urgent societal interests or the rights of children over against those of their parents—to intervene in the educational mission of free-standing schools.

CHALLENGES TO THE RIGHT OF PARENTS TO DETERMINE EDUCATION

The priority of parents in this respect was recognized in the Universal Declaration of Human Rights (1948): "parents have a prior right to choose the kind of education that shall be given to their children."[1] The distinction between instruction, as a concern shared by government, and education, as a concern exclusively of parents and the teachers they choose for their children, was made more explicit in the International Covenant on Economic, Social and Cultural Rights (1976), in which covenanting parties undertook

> to have respect for the liberty of parents . . . to choose for their children schools, other than those established by public authorities, which conform to such minimum educational standards as may be laid down or approved by the State and to ensure the religious and moral education of their children in conformity with their own convictions.[2]

The United States, it might be noted in passing, is one of the very few nations worldwide that have not ratified this covenant.

Some Western democracies, however, specify ambitious goals for both public and nonpublic schools that go well beyond knowledge and skills. For example, article 14/5a of the Austrian *Federal Constitution* devotes more than 150 words (in the English translation) to spelling out all the qualities of character that schools should promote.[3]

Similarly, Estonia expects all schools to promote "fundamental human values such as honour, care, dignity, justice, respect to oneself and others etc. and societal values such as democracy, freedom, respect to mother tongue and culture, patriotism, cultural pluralism, tolerance, economic sustainability, solidarity, rule of law, responsibility and gender equality."[4]

Spanish law insists that "[e]ducation in values should be infused into all areas of the curriculum" and defines this as including "personal freedom, responsibility, democratic citizenship, solidarity, tolerance, equality, respect, and justice."[5]

Likewise, Malta prescribes that "fundamental values of love, family, respect, inclusion, social justice, solidarity, democracy, commitment and responsibility should constitute the foundations of the compulsory educational process."[6] These and similar legal provisions reach far into the zone of parental decision-making when parents send their children to schools operated by government.

On the other hand, most Western democracies protect the right of parents to send their children to nonpublic schools, whether receiving government subsidies or not, that have their own distinctive perspectives on ultimate questions and express this through every aspect of school life. In various ways, nonpublic schools' approaches to their educational missions—their *caractère propre* (France), *richting* (Netherlands), or *ideario* (Spain)—are protected in education laws and even in some constitutions.

How real this protection is in practice is another matter, however. For example, postcommunist Romania's constitution calls for public and private schools alike to promote "the free, full and harmonious development of the human individuality, in the formation of an autonomous personality, and in assuming of a system of values necessary for personal fulfillment," with "independence from any ideologies, religious dogmas, and political doctrines, and the formation of a world view based on humanistic and scientific values."[7]

To the degree that governments seek to promote individual freedom for self-definition, they are likely to come in conflict with religious minorities that uphold traditional views on morality as a precious inheritance and seek to develop them in their young.

RECENT FLOURISHING OF JEWISH DAY SCHOOLS

During the nineteenth and early twentieth centuries, the Jewish minorities in Western Europe, as in the United States, were generally committed to assimilation and saw public schools as a primary instrument for the successful participation of their children in both society and economy. Russian Jewish immigrant Mary Antin's *The Promised Land* (1912) was a classic expression of this eager embrace of the common public school.[8]

After the catastrophe of the Holocaust, however, there was a reawakening of interest in preserving a distinctive Jewish identity and community life, and full-time Jewish schools gained increasing support. "A consensus emerged, sometimes reluctantly, that [private] day school education, once suspect as an instrument of 'segregation,' 'ghettoization,' and inferior general education, was the most effective single instrument for the maintenance of Jewish identity and the acquisition of Jewish culture and religion."[9]

As a result, the number of such schools rose dramatically. In Britain, for example, from 26 in the 1950s to 139 in 2014–2015, even as the number of Jews in Britain declined.[10] Thus,

> [i]n Britain, by 2007, a majority of all Jewish children aged 4 to 18 attended Jewish day schools, up from 20 per cent in 1975; in the United States more than a quarter of Jewish children attended day schools compared with 10 per

cent in 1975; and in France close to 40 per cent attended day schools compared with 16 per cent in 1986. [11]

The increased enrollment in Jewish schools in France (from 400 in 1945 to 32,000 in 2014, most in state-subsidized schools) has been attributed, in part, to security concerns arising from attacks by some in the Muslim population, including by classmates. An official report concluded that some schools were unsafe for Jewish children to attend. [12]

Supporters of Jewish day schools have been insistent that they should not be seen as a rejection of full participation in the surrounding society. Jewish leadership in France a century ago claimed that Jewish schools were "better at assimilating Jewish children to France than public schools, precisely because they provided religious foundations for assimilation." [13]

Such assertions have been called into question by some observers, as the proportion of Jewish schools serving "Haredi" or so-called ultra-Orthodox communities has increased, a phenomenon noted in Western Europe as well as in the United States. In Britain in 2016, 97 of the Jewish schools were "strictly Orthodox," compared with 42 considered "mainstream," [14] while in France 30 of the 50 new Jewish schools created during the 1980s and 1990s were Haredi. [15]

In Antwerp, which has a large Jewish community, there are four Haredi elementary schools for girls, five for boys, and one for pupils with special needs, as against two for non-Haredi Jewish pupils. [16] As we will see, it is these strictly Orthodox schools that sometimes come into conflict with government over their educational goals and methods, as well as over instructional content.

RESISTANCE TO GOVERNMENT SUPERVISION

Differing Instructional Goals

One form of conflict is over the adequacy of the instruction provided in the subjects prescribed by government. In New York State and in England and Israel, it has been charged that some Orthodox Jewish schools do not provide the skills and knowledge required to function successfully in contemporary society. Often the concern is directed especially at the yeshivas attended by some boys after their bar mitzvah, which focus primarily on study and discussion of religious texts. In 2016, for example, an English newspaper claimed that its investigation had

> found that more than 1,000 children are missing from schools in London and are at risk of abuse in illegal faith schools. The schools are ultra-Orthodox Jewish faith schools at which boys are placed from the age of 13, and where

they receive no education beyond studying religious texts. A number of pupils leave school with little or no ability to speak English, and few—if any—qualifications or skills which equip them to work, or live independently.[17]

According to the government, most English yeshivas are not registered as schools and are thus operating illegally and without regular inspection.[18]

In such cases, the instructional requirements of government are not being met because those who manage the schools, and the parents who entrust their sons to them, place a higher value on a sharply different concept of the knowledge and skills required for the lives that they wish them to pursue. This is not so much a conflict between instructional goals set by government and the educational goals of parents, as it is between two sets of instructional goals, each coherent on its own terms, but incompatible.

Some countries have sought to make room for alternative instructional goals. To return to the Austrian example, "[p]rivate schools with alternative curricula or deviating forms of organization will be recognized if their curricula and organization are approved by the Ministry of Education."[19]

In France, the national ministry "issues curriculum programs which public schools and private schools under *contrat d'association* [providing public funding] must follow, unless they have received approval of an experimental alternative approach."[20]

If the board of a Dutch nonpublic school "believes that one or more of the attainment targets, as formulated by the government, conflicts with its distinctive character, it may propose alternative goals for that aspect of the curriculum. If these are approved by the responsible school inspector as of the same standard as the official attainment targets, they may be implemented."[21]

The Romanian government officially recognizes various alternative pedagogies such as Freinet, Montessori, "curative pedagogy," Jena Plan, and Waldorf, and schools employing these are held to their own alternative standards.[22]

These and other countries, while adopting national curriculum standards, left room for proposals for alternative standards that were equivalent without being identical. Could such a solution be possible in the case of the yeshivas described by their critics in New York and elsewhere? Of course, the devil is in the details; what is an equivalent set of goals for the education of a member of a society? And should government representatives have exclusive authority to make that determination or should this be a matter for negotiation within a context of religious liberty?

Even when, as in Belgium, a wide scope is allowed for nongovernment schools to define their instructional goals, there may be informal pressures for conformity. "External exams are not mandatory but free-subsidized Haredi schools do participate in such exams, in order to evaluate themselves and to gain credit in anticipation of the inspection" carried out periodically by government. In a recent change, this inspection now includes the teaching of religion, previously excluded, no doubt because of the increased concern about Islamic radicalism.

In contrast with the much more numerous Catholic schools, which "maintain their pedagogical autonomy by using curricula and pupil assessments offered by their organization," some Jewish schools find themselves conforming to government standards even though not required to do so. "Haredi schools unwilling to accept these conditions opt for the independent status, which does not require them to participate in the inspection but prevents them from issuing officially recognized diplomas."[23]

Differing Educational Goals

A second, and more widespread, sort of conflict arises when a government agency, while recognizing the strong quality of the instructional program of a school, seeks to require it to promote values in conflict with the school's fundamental mission and the motivation of parents entrusting it with their children.

Such issues have arisen especially in England in recent years. It is alleged by the British Office for Standards in Education ("Ofsted"), the official school inspectorate, that some Orthodox Jewish schools are violating "British values" because the educational focus of these schools conflicts with the educational requirements of society.

For example, the publicly funded Beis Yaakov High School for Girls serves an Orthodox clientele for whom social media and smartphones are unknown entities. During an Ofsted inspection, the girls were asked questions such as "Do you have a boyfriend?"; "What do you know about men being married to each other?"; and "What do you think about Facebook?"[24]

Previous inspections had rated the school as outstanding, but "because of the pupils' bemused responses to those insensitive, inappropriate questions, the school . . . was graded as failing," with follow-up inspections every three months. Beis Yaakov was able to improve its grade by amending its curriculum "to include discussions of homosexuality and transgender issues." The distress suffered by students as a result of the continued inspections was such that the school made a formal complaint.

> Some believe that . . . [Ofsted] was not respecting the religious ethos of faith schools, indeed that these inspections were antithetical to their faith and undermined the whole basis of faith schools. Some would go further and suggest that inspectors were trying to impose a secular worldview that challenged the religious commitment of believing children.[25]

Similarly, in 2017,

> Vishnitz Girls School—where the teaching of Jewish and religious studies was singled out for praise by inspectors in its first Ofsted report of July 2013—was

presented with an ultimatum: teach your children about homosexuality and gender reassignment, or we will close you down. In the space of four years, Ofsted inspectors have now graded it as a failing school, based on this sole issue . . . to the Haredi Jewish families who send their daughters—aged three to ten—to the school, it represents an impossible dilemma. [26]

The inspectorate had found that "Pupils are not taught explicitly about issues such as sexual orientation." Ofsted's report charged that the school "restricts spiritual, moral, social and cultural development and does not take account of differing lifestyles."

A parent told the *Daily Mail* that the "mistake Ofsted has made is in thinking we have a choice in the matter, but religion is our lives, and we will not budge." For Haredi families, the "notion of teaching a seven-year-old Haredi girl about gender reassignment is anathema. Yet as far as Ofsted is concerned, Haredi schools face a simple choice: abandon a key religious principle or be closed down."[27]

In such cases government, in the name of "fundamental British values," is extending its reach beyond the barrier suggested by the distinction between instruction and education, and raising a perilous challenge to the right of parents to decide for their children about the worldview into which they will be educated.

The emphasis on enforcing "British values" is a recent development and appears to be a reaction to concern, much promoted by the media, that radical Islamists were seeking to use their positions in public schools to promote alienation from British society. Education Secretary Michael Gove, who had earlier published a book on Islamic terrorism and the weakness of Western response,[28] announced that all schools would be required to promote "British values" of tolerance and fairness.

The Orthodox Jewish schools were thus caught in the frenzy to root out radical alienation from schools. So, journalist Melanie Phillips concluded, "the Jews were to pay the price for the failings of others."

> To the secular mind, . . . all cultures that reject liberal assumptions are an equal threat to others. Recently Dame Louise Casey, who reported for the government on integration, told The Times she would scrap all faith schools that didn't teach progressive values "around our laws on women, equalities, gay marriage—all of it." Yet her view of gender roles, sexual openness or gay rights is not fundamental to British or western values. It derives from secular ideology, which is now being enforced on Charedi schools. These are not to be allowed to preserve the sexual innocence of their children. They are not to be allowed to practise their own precepts within their own unthreatening community. They are being forced to conform to secular zealotry. [. . .] A policy ostensibly against intolerance is therefore itself profoundly intolerant. The ultra-orthodox require just one thing of the state—that it leaves them alone.[29]

Soon after the controversy over the Vishnitz curriculum, Yesodey Hatorah girls' school in London came to the attention of Ofsted when its censored textbooks were obtained by Humanists UK. "In a section on the position of women in modern American society," for example, "references to women smoking, drinking and driving with men were redacted, as was the sentence: 'They kissed in public.'"[30] This school's examination results had "put it in the top 2 per cent of the country for maths and the top 10 per cent for English."

The government inspectors, according to a report in *The Telegraph*, were not interested in the school's high results and positive climate. "What they want to know about is sex. They worry that the pupils are not taught about sex. It is alleged—though also denied—that they stopped girls in the corridors and asked them intrusive questions about things like internet dating sites. They raided the library, and discovered that some of the books have passages about sex blacked out. They are angry that the girls are not taught about homosexuality."[31] Ofsted's subsequent report rated the school as "inadequate"; it had previously been rated "outstanding."

Belgian provincial authorities require that religious instruction in schools include "competencies for dialogue and living together" including shared projects with pupils from other traditions. The government required from the different recognized and taught religions *"competenties voor dialoog and samenleving"* with different kinds of common projects in order to improve the understanding between the pupils of different religious backgrounds. In Antwerp, another Haredi primary school for girls was criticized by Flemish government inspectors and official approval withdrawn for its alleged

> refusal to provide sexual education on the one hand and to bring pupils in touch with a diverse set of media on the other. [. . .] Its refusal was based on the religious conviction that sexuality is primarily situated in the private atmosphere of Jewish families, and that it is within that family context that sexual education should be taking place.[32]

The school leadership "explained that although televisions, radios, videos and internet were absent at the school, a worthy alternative was provided with PowerPoint, a media class, books, computers, papers, magazines and tape recorders." This alternative was not accepted by the inspectorate.

Some Jewish schools choose to redefine themselves as " collective homeschooling," ineligible for the government funding provided to other religious schools; their students, however, need to take the examinations set by the Ministry of Education to receive formal qualifications.

According to staff at Agudath Israel in Antwerp, "when the girls of Bais Chinuch secondary school—a collective homeschooling school—went to Brussels to take the oral A level in Dutch literature, every single girl got a cynical remark about her 'non-sexual background' and all were asked questions about the two or three sexual orientated pages of the book as if there were nothing else in that book."

Why Have Conflicts over Government Oversight Increased?

It seems likely that increased government intervention in the educational mission of Orthodox Jewish schools is largely a response to concern that Islamic schools—or Muslim educators in public schools, as in the English case—will promote in their pupils a rejection of the values and habits necessary for successful participation in Western societies.

Despite occasional troubling incidents, in fact there is little evidence that this is the case; Muslim parents who choose (and often pay for) these schools are as concerned as any other parents that their children be successful in the host society, as our Boston University team found in studying seven such schools in the United States.[33]

Such controversies are arising even in the Netherlands, which has perhaps the strongest tradition and legal protection for schools with a religious character. In March 2019, in response to a letter from the national coordinator for security and counterterrorism, the Amsterdam City Council called for the resignation of the board of a state-funded Islamic secondary school.

This school had opened in September 2017, though opposed at the time by fifteen Islamic elementary schools in the area. A spokesman for the latter charged that the school's founders were "cowboys with no eye for the public interest"; "We've been working hard to polish the image of Islamic education," he complained, "and we will not have that spoiled by a bunch of idiots."[34]

The city authorities, eighteen months later, took care to stress that their concerns about this school did not represent a general aversion to Islamic schools, which "meet an important need for parents and pupils, and that they value these schools for the quality of education they provide. Special education, including more orthodox alternatives, must be able to count on the active protection of the government. That changes when education becomes anti-democratic or undermines the principles of a democratic constitutional state, or when there are links with extremist groups." But, city authorities declared, it was

> unacceptable that there are signs young pupils are being substantially influenced by 'guiding individuals' who have been in a radical environment. . . .
> The safe and democratic education of Amsterdam students at the Cornelius Haga Lyceum cannot be guaranteed while the school is promoting a parallel society and acting in a way that is contrary to the government's anti-radicalisation strategy.[35]

This situation, and reports of resistance to government inspection, led to more than five hours of debate in the Dutch Parliament over how the school could be closed, given the strong protections for faith-based schools under Dutch law.[36] While the storm over this school seems to have abated, at least for the moment, a leading Dutch education law expert suggests, in a private communication, that the extensive latitude traditionally granted to faith-based schools in the Netherlands is now under threat.

"This doesn't mean," he wrote me, "there is a majority for a system with only state schools. What is happening however, in the framework of official policy, is that a lot of legal measures that in former days were designed to protect religious schools specifically, will be cancelled in the near future. The discussion about the Islamic schools seems to accelerate this process."[37]

Similarly, the French minister of education, in 2016, warned that the children of immigrants were being radicalized in Islamic schools, schools that, she said, were animated by "confessional mobilization hostile to the values of the Republic." This charge led, in turn, to legislation adopted in April 2018 increasing the authority of local and national government to prevent such schools from opening.

THREATS TO THE INSTRUCTION/EDUCATION DISTINCTION

In Western Europe, the long-standing policy compromise—leaving it up to parents and their chosen schools to determine how their children are educated so long as minimal government standards are met—is facing a serious challenge.

This challenge is clearly related to the perceived threat of Islamic jihadism. No one is seriously worried that Orthodox Jews (or Conservative Protestants and Catholics), no matter how out of sympathy with majority cultural norms, will become dangerously militant, but it is difficult to increase scrutiny of the character-forming activities of Islamic schools without extending that scrutiny to other faith traditions.

This increased scrutiny of independent schools by government will inevitably extend into domains of values and worldview that have been considered the responsibility of families and of civil society institutions and not subject to government regulation. This burden will not fall equally on schools operating on the basis of different perspectives. For example, it should cause little difficulty for schools offering "humanistic education" in the Netherlands by helping pupils to learn how to make decisions for themselves. This emphasis on individualistic autonomy is entirely consistent with the norms of a society based on consumerism and self-definition.

Supporters of conservative Protestant education, on the other hand, regard this as wishful thinking based upon a view of human nature that denies its potential for evil. Simply leaving pupils to make decisions as best they can, helping them only with the (ostensibly neutral) process of decision-making independent of external authorities, leaves them utterly vulnerable to the influence of the values abroad in society.

It is not as though pupils were likely to invent authentically original values for themselves; during the stage when they tend to reject whatever their parents stand for, they are very likely to act on the basis of the values presented to them in the media and by their peer group. Thus these Protestant (and Catholic and Jewish and Muslim) educators seek to relate pupils to a coherent tradition of moral intuitions and conduct.

In order to equip young people to be competent decision-makers, leaders in faith-based schools believe, it is important to provide them with an alternative way of understanding the world and arriving at decisions, so that they will not be overwhelmed by the influence of what seems absolutely taken for granted in the surrounding culture. The school should help pupils to learn to see with eyes that are not dazzled by the images presented to them by the wider society.

What seems to be occurring in a number of countries is a growing anxiety about the erosion of shared values and a determination to use popular schooling—including that in faith-based schools—to promote social unity. The massive immigration from predominantly Muslim countries, and the populist reaction against this and other social changes, are leading governments to seek to use schools to achieve what François Guizot, in the 1830s, called "a certain government of minds."[38]

This strategy, if pressed too vigorously, will be a profound threat to religious freedom. In response to the Yesodey Hatorah controversy, one commentator argued that "what we mean by 'British values' is at stake here, and whether such values are generous enough to include groups such as the Haredim."[39]

It is difficult to understand how the determination of a small and self-isolating religious group to raise its children according to traditional moral and sexual norms poses a threat to the wider society of Britain or any other nation. How ironic that, only a couple of generations after liberation from imposed religious orthodoxies, society should be subjected to persecutions on the basis of newly defined sexual orthodoxies!

NOTES

1. Alfred Fernandez and Siegfried Jenkner, "International Declarations and Conventions on the Right to Education and the Freedom of Education," Article 26, Section 3 (Frankfurt am Main: Info3-Verlag, 1995).

2. Ibid., Article 13, Section 3.

3. Walter Berka and Charles Glenn, "Austria," in *Balancing Freedom, Autonomy, and Accountability in Education*, eds. Charles L. Glenn and Jan De Groof, vol. 2 (Tilburg: Wolf Legal Publishers, 2012), 25.

4. Merilin Kiviorg, "Estonia," in *Balancing Freedom, Autonomy, and Accountability in Education*, eds. Charles L. Glenn and Jan De Groof, vol. 2 (Tilburg: Wolf Legal Publishers, 2012), 165.

5. Arturo Galán and Charles Glenn, "Spain," in *Balancing Freedom, Autonomy, and Accountability in Education*, eds. Charles L. Glenn and Jan De Groof, vol. 2 (Tilburg: Wolf Legal Publishers), 510.

6. Christopher Bezzina, "Malta," in *Balancing Freedom, Autonomy, and Accountability in Education*, eds. Charles L. Glenn and Jan De Groof, vol. 2 (Tilburg: Wolf Legal Publishers), 340.

7. Raluca Bigu, "Romania," in *Balancing Freedom, Autonomy, and Accountability in Education*, eds. Charles L. Glenn and Jan De Groof, vol. 2 (Tilburg: Wolf Legal Publishers), 459.

8. Mary Antin, *The Promised Land* (New York: Penguin Classics, 1912).

9. Zvi Gitelman, "Do Jewish Schools Make a Difference in the Former Soviet Union?," in *Jewish Day Schools, Jewish Communities: A Reconsideration*, eds. Alex Pomson and Howard Deitcher (Portland: The Littman Library of Jewish Civilization, 2007), 112.

10. Simon Rocker, "The Unstoppable Rise of Jewish Schools," *The Jewish Chronicle*, November 17, 2016, https://www.thejc.com/education/education-features/%20the-unstoppable%20-rise-of-jewish-schools-1.54925.

11. Alex Pomson, "Introduction: Jewish Schools, Jewish Communities: A Reconsideration," in *Jewish Day Schools, Jewish Communities: A Reconsideration*, eds. Alex Pomson and Howard Deitcher (Portland: The Littman Library of Jewish Civilization), 2.

12. Denis Peiron, "Pourquoi les Familles Juives Désertent des Écoles Publiques," *La Croix*, November 3, 2016, https://www.la-croix.com/Religion/Judaisme/%20Pourquoi-familles%20-juives-desertent-ecoles-publiques-2016-03-11-1200745971.

13. John R. Bowen, *Can Islam Be French? Pluralism and Pragmatism in a Secularist State* (Princeton: Princeton University Press, 2011), 181–82.

14. Rocker, "The Unstoppable Rise of Jewish Schools."

15. Kimberly A. Arkin, 2014, "The Vanishing State: Religious Education and Intolerance in French Jewish Schools," in *Religious Education and the Challenge of Pluralism*, ed. Adam B. Seligman (Oxford: Oxford University Press), 100.

16. Lotem Perry-Hazan, "From the Constitution to the Classroom: Educational Freedom in Antwerp's Ultra-Orthodox Jewish Schools," *Journal of School Choice* 8, no. 3 (2014): 481, https://doi.org/10.1080/15582159.2014.942178.

17. Siobhan Fenton, "An Investigation by *The Independent* Reveals Thousands of Children in London Have Been Moved to Unregistered Ultra-Orthodox Jewish Schools," *The Independent*, Sunday, April 3, 2016, https://www.independent.co.uk/news/uk/home-news/%20illegal-jewish-schools-department-of-education-knew-about-council-%20faith-school-cover-%20up-as-thousands-a6965516.

18. Fran Abrams, "Why Are Orthodox Jewish Religious Schools Unregulated?," *The Guardian*, August 11, 2015, https://www.theguardian.com/education/2015/aug/11/orthodox-jewish-religious-schools-unregulated-london-yeshiva.

19. Berka and Glenn, "Austria," 5, 8.

20. André Legrand and Charles Glenn, "France," in *Balancing Freedom, Autonomy, and Accountability in Education*, eds. Charles L. Glenn and Jan De Groof, vol. 2 (Tilburg: Wolf Legal Publishers), 202.

21. Paul Zoontjens and Charles Glenn, "The Netherlands," in *Balancing Freedom, Autonomy, and Accountability in Education*, eds. Charles L. Glenn and Jan De Groof, vol. 2 (Tilburg: Wolf Legal Publishers).

22. Bigu, "Romania."

23. Perry-Hazan, "From the Constitution to the Classroom: Educational Freedom in Antwerp's Ultra-Orthodox Jewish Schools."

24. Richard Price, "Jewish School Faces Closure for Refusing to Teach Its Young Girls Transgender Issues Despite Its Religious Ethos Being Praised Four Years Ago," *Daily Mail*, July 13, 2017, https://www.dailymail.co.uk/news/article-4694610/School-faces-closure-refusing-transgender-issues.html.

25. James Arthur, "Extremism and Neo-Liberal Education Policy: A Contextual Critique of the Trojan Horse Affair in Birmingham Schools," *British Journal of Educational Studies* 63, no. 3 (September 2015): 323.

26. Price, "Jewish School Faces Closure."

27. Ibid.

28. Michael Gove, *Celsius 7/7* (London: Weidenfeld and Nicholson, 2006).

29. Melanie Phillips, "Schools Pay the Price for the Failings of Others," *Jewish Chronicle*, March 28, 2018, https://www.thejc.com/comment/columnists/charedi-schools-extremism-melanie-phillips-ofsted-louise-casey-1.461467.

30. Sarah Marsh, "Jewish School Removed 'Homosexual' Mentions from GCSE Textbook: Yesodey Hatorah Girls' School in London Also Censored Images of Women Socialising with Men," *The Guardian*, March 5, 2018, https://www.theguardian.com/education/ 2018/mar/09/ yesodey-hatorah-jewish-girls-school-north-london-homosexual-references-textbook.

31. Charles Moore, "In the Battle Between Equality and Religion, Must Religion Always Lose?," *The Telegraph*, April 6, 2018, https://www.telegraph.co.uk/politics/2018/04/06/ battle-equality-religion-must-religion-always-lose/.

32. Johan Lievens, "All Education Is Free, but Some Initiatives Are Freer Than Others: The End of Jewish Education in Flanders?," unpublished conference paper, 2018, 8.

33. Charles L. Glenn, *Muslim Educators in American Communities* (Charlotte: Information Age, 2018).

34. Janene Pieters, "Islamic Primary Schools Against New Islamic High School in Amsterdam," *NL Times*, July 31, 2017, https://nltimes.nl/2017/07/31/islamic-primary-schools-new-islamic-high-school-amsterdam.

35. City of Amsterdam, "The City of Amsterdam Wants Board Haga Lyceum to Step Down," March 14, 2019.

36. Zack Newmark, "Amsterdam School Director Threatened the Education Inspectorate," March 15, 2019, https://nltimes.nl/2019/03/15/amsterdam-school-director-threatened-education-inspectorate.

37. Paul Zoontjens, private communication, April 7, 2019.

38. Charles L. Glenn, *The Myth of the Common School* (Amherst: University of Massachusetts Press, 1988): 36.

39. Giles Fraser, "Why Is Ofsted Doing the Secularists' Bidding?," *UnHerd*, March 22, 2018, https://unherd.com/2018/03/ofsted-secularists-bidding/.

Part Three

Implications for Different Communities

Chapter Seven

"Substantial Equivalency"

Implications for the Jewish Community

Avi Schick

Since November 2018, New York's private school community has been at odds with the New York State Education Department (NYSED) about guidelines and regulations that would impact the instruction, schedule, and staffing at independent and religious schools.

Tens of thousands of parents and alumni signed petitions urging the (now former) education commissioner to walk back guidelines issued on November 20, 2018, and a coalition of more than one thousand Catholic, Jewish, and independent schools sued the state education department to block them from being implemented. After those lawsuits were successful and the guidelines were struck down, more than 140,000 advocates submitted public comments urging the board of regents to reject the nearly identical regulations that were proposed to replace them.

The goal of this essay is twofold. It seeks to explain what will happen if the regulations proposed by NYSED are enacted. In doing so, it will also explain why the guidelines and regulations have been so vigorously opposed.

To understand what is at stake, it is useful to contrast two statements. The first formed the basis for a landmark U.S. Supreme Court decision (*Pierce v. Society of Sisters*, 268 U.S. 510) nearly a century ago: "A child is not the mere creature of the State; those who nurture him and direct his destiny have the right, coupled with the high duty, to recognize and prepare him for additional obligations."

The second was offered on April 15, 2019, by the assistant attorney general defending the guidelines issued by NYSED. He argued to Albany Supreme Court Justice Christina Ryba that the guidelines were necessary to protect the "voiceless child who can be conscripted at their parents will" to attend a religious school.[1]

These two statements reflect diametrically opposed worldviews. One posits that parents have rights superior to those of the state when it comes to directing the education and upbringing of their children. The other casts the educational choices parents make for their children in terms more commonly used to describe involuntary army service.

At bottom, then, this is a battle about control. Will parents be permitted to set the educational direction for their children? Do the leaders of the private schools chosen by parents have the final word on matters of instruction, direction, mission, and hiring, or does the state?

For yeshivas in particular, the loss of control and of their independence would be crippling. Several reasons why this is so will be explored in the next section. Before we get there, it is useful to review a prior attempt to transform New York yeshivas by means of a reinterpretation of the compulsory education law.

On March 17, 1939, the New York State Board of Regents adopted a resolution that read, in its entirety:

> *Voted*, That private or parochial schools that operate with a program providing a session carried on in a foreign language during the forenoon, with only an afternoon session in English, be advised that such practice violates the compulsory education law.[2]

At that time, there were no Hasidic yeshivas in New York, nor were there more than a few that could be deemed Haredi. They all offered instruction in the core secular studies subjects. Yet that was not enough for the board of regents, which sought to have yeshivas mimic the schedule of the public schools.

All twenty-six yeshivas then in existence banded together to fight the resolution and its implementation, which they viewed as an existential threat to their mission. At a hearing in July 1942, the yeshivas expressed concerns that the potential regulations represented, in the words of Yiddish journalist Ephraim Caplan, "a destruction of the Torah, for a harsh decree of the Board of Regents would bring destruction to the Yeshivas, would annihilate the fortress of our spiritual existence."[3]

In exploring the impact these regulations would have on Jewish education, it is necessary to acknowledge the singular value and virtue of Torah study in Jewish life, and the role that yeshivas play in transmitting Torah and its values to Jewish children.

To use Caplan's terminology, yeshivas are our fortresses and Torah study is our spiritual existence.

MORE REGULATION MEANS LESS TORAH STUDY

If the proposed regulations are adopted and enforced, the primary consequence will be a diminution in the study of Torah. There are only so many hours in the school day, and a requirement to devote an increased number of them to secular studies necessarily means that fewer will be devoted to studying Torah.

For Orthodox parents, yeshiva education is the vehicle by which they satisfy biblical commands that are at the core of Jewish life. As Deuteronomy 11:18–19 commands, "You shall place these words of Mine upon your heart and upon your soul . . . and you shall teach them to your children to speak in them."

Parents who live by this command are following the example of Abraham, about whom the Bible writes, "I have known him because he commands his sons and his household after him, that they should keep the way of the Lord."[4]

During prayers recited daily, Orthodox Jews acknowledge the obligation to discuss the Torah and its commandments "when we lay down and when we get up . . . for they are our life, and the entire length of our days, and we will think about them day and night."

As recounted in Prophets (Joshua 1:8): "The book of the Torah shall not depart from your mouth; you should contemplate it day and night so that you may observe all that is written there, for then your ways will be successful and your actions wise."

Yeshivas help parents fulfill these commandments and dictates by providing their children with an education that is rooted in Jewish texts, laws, and values informed by Jewish morality, history, culture, ideals, and aspirations.

There is surely more than one opinion about the number of hours of Torah study necessary to satisfy these biblical dictates. Different rabbis and communities can and have come to different conclusions about what they require. Nevertheless, such fundamental religious matters are surely not the prerogative of the bureaucrats in the state education department or the members of the board of regents. And yet if these regulations were adopted, they would become the primary authority regulating the number of hours Jewish children in New York can devote to the study of Torah.

That cannot be.

NYSED's proposed regulations would require all private and parochial elementary schools to teach twelve required courses to students at each grade level. In the upper elementary grades, both the rejected guidance and the proposed regulations would require that at least 17.5 hours a week must be devoted to these classes.

The typical yeshiva teaches secular studies subjects four afternoons (Monday through Thursday) per week. The state is therefore seeking to require that 4.4 hours of secular studies instruction be offered each of those four weekday afternoons—more than currently offered by the vast majority of New York yeshivas. These newly required hours devoted to secular studies will come at the expense of Torah study.

Government rules that hinder religious study and observance are subject to the most stringent standard of review, known in the legal system as "strict scrutiny." To survive strict scrutiny, the rule or regulation in question must (i) advance a compelling state interest; (ii) be narrowly tailored to further that goal; and (iii) use the least restrictive means to achieve its purpose.

Whatever legitimate interest the government may have in education generally, New York has offered no rationale to justify the particular requirements of its guidance and regulations. The guidelines and regulations would make private schools the curricular clones of their public school counterparts, but a desire to homogenize education across private and public schools is certainly an insufficient basis for regulation.

The state has never even attempted to explain why the particular course list is necessary, or why each subject must be taught for the precise length of time prescribed by the regulations. The state's exclusive focus on inputs—on what to teach, how to teach it, and how long it must be taught—while ignoring outputs (what the students know) and outcomes (what they do after they graduate) should prove fatal under strict scrutiny.

Nor is there anything in the proposed regulations for parents, schools, and communities that measure success not by the median income of their alumni but by their moral and character development, the values they live by, the faith they adhere to, the Torah they study, the families they build, and the communal bonds they sustain.

None of this is surprising. In the secular state we inhabit, government does not even consider let alone credit values that are seen as spiritual or religious. Producing hardworking, law-abiding graduates who lead stable families in New York *should* be recognized by the state as a civic good that contributes to its well-being. But these are not the virtues the state values when assessing the religious students and graduates of New York's yeshivas, and so the state neither measures nor credits them.

The secular state is only half of the problem. In a more tolerant world, values and choices that are not shared would still be respected. But the ascendance of the paternalistic nanny state, in which government dictates what conduct is required or forbidden in ever-expanding spheres of our lives, makes that impossible.

The regulations reflect the worst of all worlds for religious parents and community—the convergence of the secular state and the nanny state. The result is a state that sees no value in religious education and has no inclination to defer to parents. It is a state that may soon be inhospitable to religious education, parents, and communities.

There is an additional reason that the regulations are untenable.

Torah study in a yeshiva setting is indisputably the key to Jewish continuity. In a seminal essay by Rabbi Haym Soloveitchik, he observes that:

> In contemporary society . . . Jewish identity is not inevitable. It is not a matter of course, but of choice: a conscious preference of the enclave over the host society. For such a choice to be made, a sense of particularity and belonging must be instilled by intentional enterprise of instruction. Without education there is no identity, for identity in a multi-culture is ideological. Identity maintenance and consciousness raising are needs that can be met only by education. [5]

It was not always so. As Professor Jack Wertheimer has explained,

> The day schools of the 20th century are unique, however, in the mission they have been assigned. . . . Up to the middle of the 20th century, it was widely assumed by Jews of all stripes that Jewishness was something almost innate, and no school was needed to inculcate it. . . . Until midcentury, the children of immigrants on the right [of the Orthodox world] imbibed their religiosity primarily from home and ethnic neighborhood, much as children of their far more numerous brethren on the left and center imbibed their Jewishness from much the same sources. The inability of families to play their accustomed roles and the collapse of ethnic neighborhoods necessitated the creation of a new type of day school movement. [6]

Orthodox Jewish practice and life has seen an almost miraculous resurgence and growth since the destruction of the Holocaust. Torah study and ritual observance can be found all across the United States.

When World War II ended in 1945, between 6,000 and 7,000 New York students enrolled in roughly 30 K–12 yeshivas and Jewish day schools. [7] As recently as 2018, there were nearly 165,000 students enrolled in approximately 440 K–12 yeshivas and day schools across New York State. [8]

The increase in yeshiva enrollment is not a consequence of that rebirth, it is the cause of it. If Jewish education is weakened, if the vision of school leaders is diluted, if their authority is undermined, Jewish life in the United States will suffer. A diminished focus on the study of Jewish texts, laws, rituals, history, and ideals will result in graduates with a concomitant diminished commitment to lifelong Torah study and ritual observance.

As Dr. Marvin Schick has explained:

> Jewish schools have a dual curriculum and a dual mission. One purpose is education. The other is religious socialization, the process whereby young children are taught to understand and accept the principles of our faith. This mission transcends courses and curriculum but does require substantial time during the school day, time that under the proposed regulations would need to be shifted away from Jewish studies. [9]

Numerous academic studies have concluded that attending a yeshiva or day school as a child is the factor that most significantly determines whether one will observe Jewish traditions and be involved in Jewish life as an adult. A study published by the Avi Chai Foundation in 1993 concluded that:

> Nine years of Jewish education appears to be a turning point in connecting Jewish education with Jewish involvement; and Jewish day schools are the best vehicle for implementing Jewish involvement and are the only type of Jewish education that stands against the very rapidly growing rate of intermarriage. [10]

Brandeis professor Sylvia Barack Fishman reached a similar conclusion after reviewing the data collected for the National Jewish Population Survey:

> Extensive Jewish education is definitively associated with every measure of adult Jewish identification. Its impact can be clearly seen in every public and private Jewish life. Younger American Jewish adults (25–44) who have received six or more years of Jewish education are the group most likely to join, volunteer time for, and donate money to Jewish causes, to belong to synagogues and attend services at least several times a year, to seek out Jewish neighborhoods and Jewish friends, to perform Jewish rituals in their homes, to visit and care deeply about Israel, and to marry another Jew. And they are the group most likely to continue the pattern and to provide many years of Jewish education to their children. [11]

Immersive Torah study is the key to Jewish continuity. NYSED's proposed regulations would tinker with the formula that yeshivas have successfully used for more than a century.

NYSED may not be concerned that altering a yeshiva's curriculum and schedule will alter the lifelong impact that it has on its students, but that is not a risk that New York's Jewish community can afford to take.

REGULATING YESHIVA INSTRUCTION WILL LEAD TO REGULATING YESHIVA VALUES

NYSED's proposed regulations are not confined to instruction in core subjects such as English, math, social studies, and science. There are at least eight additional required classes, including theater, dance, arts, career and occupational studies, and consumer and family science.

By extending far beyond the foundational courses, NYSED has signaled, intentionally or otherwise, that it intends to fill an entire curriculum. This is quite concerning to yeshivas and other parochial schools.

The most immediate concern is that the state will obligate private schools to teach values that are inimical to the religious values that are at the core of the school's mission. "Family science" may already be such a course, although the proposed regulations are vague—in a way that the November 2018 guidelines were not—about what precisely the government must be included in a "family science" curriculum.

In a 2019 op-ed, Rabbi Yaakov Bender, the dean of the highly regarded Yeshiva Darchei Torah in Far Rockaway, Queens, warned that "however well-intentioned New York's regulators of today may be, history teaches that once the autonomy of independent and religious schools is undermined, the reach of the state will only expand" so that "control over the academic curriculum today will lead to control over the values we teach tomorrow."[12]

Commenting on the state's "offer" to have local school districts evaluate a yeshiva's Jewish studies classes, Rabbi Bender observed that "an evaluation today will lead to a suggestion tomorrow and a mandate down the road."

It is not just the yeshiva community that is concerned about the state's encroachment into their values. After the NYSED guidelines were released, the Archdiocese of New York opined, "Every school has a culture of its own that is a profound influence over the children. Religious schools reinforce the faith in every activity, including in the teaching of secular subjects. Moral values are taught not just by instruction, but by example. Religious parents want their kids to grow up in that kind of environment."[13]

Yeshivas, however, may have particular cause for concern. Over the past several years, British regulators have sought to penalize yeshivas in England for reasons that are wholly unrelated to academics but are instead rooted in their Orthodox Jewish culture and religious values.

In 2017, one all-girls Orthodox elementary school was deemed "inadequate" by the U.K. Office for Standards in Education (Ofsted). By their own admission, there was nothing lacking in the *academic* instruction the girls were receiving. Rather, Ofsted faulted the school for supposedly having failed to impart "British values" to its students, which, Ofsted explained, meant that the students did not receive "a well-rounded education" nor obtain "a full understanding of the world." In this case, "British values" meant teaching students the secular-progressive views on questions of sexual orientation and gender identity.[14]

Likewise, in 2019, Ofsted rated the King David High School in Manchester as "inadequate," despite the school previously being deemed "outstanding." Once again, the reason for the poor grade had nothing to do with academics. The problem, according to Ofsted, was that King David offered different curricula in their separate boys and girls schools.

The school was criticized for making "separate educational and social arrangements for pupils in different sections of the school," which Ofsted argued meant that students "suffer detriment" on the basis of their gender.[15]

New York yeshivas have not yet experienced the kind of intrusive, nonacademic intervention and overreach felt by their counterparts in England. But if the proposed regulations were enacted, it is likely and perhaps even inevitable that the state itself and others will eventually make the same type of demands as Ofsted has.

The proposed regulations essentially require every private and parochial school to obtain a license to operate from its local school district, and to renew that license by reinspection every five years. Local jurisdictions are even more likely than the state to try to mandate that private schools teach certain values. New York City's Department of Education is already heavily focused on the cultural aspects of education. It is unfortunately too easy to envision New York City imposing "values" requirements on religious and independent schools operating within its borders.

Even if they do not impose mandatory instruction of values, local school districts may begin to factor into their evaluation of private schools whether they are teaching or adhering to progressive values.

There is only one way to ensure that the state does not infringe on the core religious values and teachings of parochial schools: to establish that the school and not the state has the final word on its educational agenda, curriculum, and pedagogical methods.

EXACERBATING TENSIONS BETWEEN COMMUNITIES

The regulations proposed by the NYSED are chock-full of requirements, dictates, enforcement mechanisms, and threatened punishments. Yet such regulations alone do not magically produce higher educational quality or attainment. If it were that easy, the highly regulated public schools would have improved long ago.

Directives that are disconnected from the culture they inhabit are meaningless. Rules that do not take into account the realities of those they affect will be ignored. State and local education officials have a hard enough time ensuring the quality of schools they directly oversee and manage. Private schools are even less likely to transform their educational philosophy and practices simply because of directives emanating from Albany. They are more likely to litigate, go underground, or engage in civil disobedience than they are to abandon their deeply held convictions to placate the government.

Where the regulations are most likely to have an impact is in the political realm. They will be used as a wedge—as they already are—by those interested in stereotyping Orthodox and Hasidic Jews as people beyond the pale of polite society.

Here too history is repeating itself. Commenting on the 1942 attempt of the board of regents to transform yeshiva education, Ephraim Caplan noted that:

> Educational institutions cannot grow in an atmosphere which regards them as lawbreakers. It is indeed regrettable, indeed grievous, that the Yeshivas which

are interested in deepening and spreading the understanding of the Torah in its students and which aim to awaken in their students justice honestly, love and loyalty . . . that these institutions for an instant should be placed in the light of violators of the law.[16]

The Haredi communities have made enormous investments to build communal institutions and infrastructure in New York. Their yeshiva system is at the center of those efforts. Yet those very yeshivas are now being used in an effort to cast them as a backward people, as a community that does not deserve a seat at the table, as a people who do not fulfill their basic civic obligations.

Make no mistake: critics are using the unique mission and educational approach of yeshivas to marginalize Orthodox Jews. And they are attracting support from people who are entirely ignorant about yeshiva education. Too many people in the education bureaucracy in New York express strong views about yeshiva education despite their never having spent any time in a yeshiva—even to visit or observe. They often attempt to excuse that failure by explaining that they are familiar with Catholic schools. They do not understand that a yeshiva's dual curriculum, dual faculty, and intensive text-based analysis looks nothing like a modern Catholic school.

The willingness of state education officials to upend yeshiva education without even bothering to first understand it has eroded what had been a cooperative relationship with the Haredi community. The Haredi community is understandably protective of what it perceives as its crown jewel, a privately built school system, maintained at great expense, that is the lifeblood of Jewish continuity. Attacks on this system, with its sky-high attendance and graduation rates, and tens of thousands of successful graduates are especially misplaced coming from those who are responsible for New York's challenged public schools to which few would aspire to be "substantially equivalent."

The result of all of this will be that Haredi and other Orthodox Jews, who have traditionally shied away from criticism of the public schools, are much more likely to become vocal about the public school failures in their backyards. After all, "substantial equivalence" invites a discussion about schools on both sides of that equation.

This tension will not be good for anyone. It will do nothing for education, and it will drive Orthodox Jews further from the very mainstream of society that education reformers supposedly want them to embrace.

Since NYSED first proposed regulations on yeshivas, the incredibly diverse (and infamously fractious) Jewish community has banded together to challenge them. There was a similarly united front eighty years ago, when the state last sought to transform yeshiva education. It took three years for the state to abandon that effort.

Let's hope that it will not take that long for New York State to get it right this time around.

NOTES

1. Marvin Schick, "As New York Once Again Targets Religious Schools, a History Lesson in Communal Resistance," *Tablet Magazine*, August 12, 2019, https://www.tabletmag.com/jewish-news-and-politics/289450/new-york-targets-religious-schools.

2. Cited in Schick, 2019.

3. Unpublished account by Ephraim Caplan, cited in Schick, 2019.

4. Genesis 18:19.

5. Haym Soloveitchik, "Rupture and Reconstruction: The Transformation of Contemporary Orthodoxy," *Tradition* 28, no. 4 (Summer 1994), http://www.lookstein.org/professional-dev/rupture-reconstruction-transformation-contemporary-orthodoxy/.

6. Jack Wertheimer, "Jewish Education in the United States: Recent Trends and Issues," *American Jewish Year Book*, American Jewish Committee, Jewish Publication Society (1999): https://www.bjpa.org/search-results/publication/17626.

7. Ibid.

8. Elya Brudny and Yisroel Reisman, "New York State Targets Jewish Schools," *Wall Street Journal*, December 13, 2018, https://www.wsj.com/articles/new-york-state-targets-jewish-schools-11544745611.

9. Schick, 2019.

10. Mordechai Rimor and Elihu Katz, "Jewish Involvement of the Baby Boom Generation," *Avi Chai*, November 1993.

11. Sylvia Barack Fishman, "Jewish Education and Jewish Identity among Contemporary American Jews: Suggestions from Current Research," Bureau of Jewish Education (Boston: Center for Educational Research and Evaluation, 1995).

12. Yaakov Bender, "State Rules Ignore Special Mission of Jewish Schools," *Albany Times Union*, January 20, 2019, https://www.timesunion.com/opinion/article/Commentary-State-rules-ignore-special-mission-of-13547036.php.

13. Ed Mechmann, "Religious Schools Are Under Attack," New York: Archdiocese of New York, December 14, 2018, https://archny.org/news/religious-schools-are-under-attack.

14. Richard Price, "Jewish School Faces Closure for Refusing to Teach Its Young Girls Transgender Issues Despite Its Religious Ethos Being Praised Four Years Ago," *Daily Mail*, July 13, 2017, https://www.dailymail.co.uk/news/article-4694610/School-faces-closure-refusing-transgender-issues.html.

15. Humanists UK, "Ofsted Slams Jewish School for Segregating Boys and Girls," June 15, 2019, https://humanism.org.uk/2019/06/15/ofsted-slams-jewish-school-for-segregating-boys-and-girls/.

16. Cited in Schick, 2019.

Chapter Eight

The Philosophical Futility of "Substantial Equivalency" in the Interplay of Religious and Public Education

A Christian School Perspective

Jay Ferguson

Early in 2019, the New York Supreme Court in Albany ruled on a challenge by several organizations—the New York Catholic Diocese, a group of parents organized to promote yeshiva education, and the New York State Association of Independent Schools—unified against the New York State Education Department's new guidelines for private education.

One of the primary issues behind the petitioners' challenge was a state requirement that religious private education in New York be "substantially equivalent" to state-sponsored schools, enforceable through inspections by local public school superintendents, and with precious little guidance as to what the term "substantially equivalent" might mean.

Christian private education is a unique enterprise, proceeding from a philosophy unique to the tenets of the faith. Philosophical and, specifically, epistemic presuppositions undergirding Christian education in America, when compared with those framing public education, render each system "substantially *non*-equivalent," or dissimilar, from the other.

Therefore, for the state to impose a "substantial equivalency" framework upon Christian schooling (and presumably other religious schooling options with disparate philosophical underpinnings) would not only fundamentally alter the nature and character of Christian schools, but in so doing, would effectively undermine and subvert the legitimate state interest in promoting a well-equipped citizenry and the common good.

While this chapter explores the philosophic problems inherent in attempting to inspect Christian schools by those operating from a public school epistemic paradigm, the same arguments could, and should, be considered through the framework of *any* system of religious private education. Further, these arguments could credibly be extended to *all* independent schools, which by their charters and marketplace dynamics are inherently distinctive from and dissimilar to their public counterparts.

EPISTEMIC FORK IN THE ROAD . . .

The epistemic divergence of public and Christian private schools was not always as dramatic as today. The common school movement in America had its roots in Christian Protestantism, albeit of a generalized, homogenized sort. While the initial Protestant ethos of the common school movement was arguably never particularly or distinctively Christian in focus, certainly by the mid-twentieth century, under the influence of two world wars and the Progressivism era, the unitary state school system lost whatever Protestant or orthodox Christian flavor it had once had.[1]

By the 1940s and 1950s, public schools were haunted by what Robert Bellah called "Civil Religion," a kind of "God-and-country" religion or ceremonial deism, long departed from orthodox Christianity, with basic, generic tenets: the existence of God, the life to come, rewards for virtue and punishment for vice, and the exclusion of religious intolerance.[2] State-sponsored prayers were still offered at the start of the day in many schools, and the Bible read in class, but as a kind of quasi-religious act of patriotism, similar to the Pledge of Allegiance.

Two seminal U.S. Supreme Court cases on prayer and Bible reading in schools extended the long-implied Establishment Clause doctrine of "separation of church and state" to create a public school education system devoid of religious trappings.

In *Engel v. Vitale*, the court held that recitation of a nonsectarian prayer composed by the New York State Board of Regents violated the Establishment Clause. Justice Black, writing for the majority, said that, "neither the power nor the prestige of the . . . government would be used to control, support, or influence the kinds of prayer the American people can say—that the people's religions must not be subjected to the pressures of government."[3]

One year later, in the companion cases of *School District of Abington Township v. Schempp* and *Murray v. Curlett*, the court held that opening the school day with Bible reading was also an Establishment Clause violation. In his dissent, Justice Stewart opined that the unwritten constitutional standard of separation of church and state was a "sterile metaphor" that, "by its very nature may distort, rather than illumine, the problems involved in a particular case."

Stewart voiced concern that, given the large percentages of childhood invested in schooling, rendering religious exercises impermissible within the school day would put religion at an artificial and state-created disadvantage for children, having the practical effect of establishing a state religion of secularism or, at the very least, showing preference to those who believe religious exercises should be performed only in private.[4]

Following *Engel* and *Schempp*, any vestiges of what could conceivably be construed as state sanction of religious influence were declared unconstitutional through a series of decisions, including *Lee v. Weismann* (school-sponsored prayer by invited clergy at commencement ceremony caused state-sponsored religious coercion), and *Santa Fe Independent School District v. Doe* (student-sponsored prayer at football games or other school events constitutes state-sponsored religious coercion).

Public school officials, responding to what had truly become a judicially-sanctioned wall of separation between church and state, mostly acting in good faith and in an abundance of caution in avoiding litigation, have furthered this separation, rendering it essentially absolute.[5]

Whether or not secularism is itself religion is certainly a matter of dispute. What is not disputed, however, is that the practical effect of *Engel*, *Schempp*, and the historical development of the public school system leading up to and in the wake of those decisions, renders the American public school system undeniably secular.

By providing a common education for the broadest possible ecumenical base, coupled with the legally imposed need to divest itself of vestiges of religious affiliation, the American public school system has necessarily embraced the common philosophic/epistemic denominator required to accomplish those purposes: a secular, naturalistic epistemology. Herein lie the seeds of substantial dissimilarity with religious education generally, and Christian education specifically.

... AND NEVER THE TWAIN SHALL MEET

The purposes of Christian education stretch beyond those of its public counterpart. Christian education does not seek merely to impart knowledge or encourage character in its students. First and foremost, and at its best, Christian education seeks to shape the heart of a people, giving them a vision of the good life, a life manifested within the gospel of Jesus Christ, and to instill in them the passion to pursue that vision. "The primary goal of Christian education is the formation of a peculiar people—a people who desire the kingdom of God and thus undertake their vocations as an expression of that desire."[6]

For education to be truly Christian, it must teach and form the students entrusted to its care to think and feel Christianly.[7] To reach these intended purposes, it must embrace an epistemic foundation and philosophy that is uniquely Christian, rooted in a vision of the world and creation as revealed in the Bible, the totality of the Old and New Testaments. These philosophies are radically different (and seen by most as opposed) to those ends and philosophies inherent in American public education.

First, and perhaps most profoundly, a Christian perception of reality conceives of what philosopher Charles Taylor calls an "enchanted" realm, not in the sense of fairies and elves, but of angelic beings, of spirits, demons, and moral forces beyond ourselves.[8]

While those who eschew similar worldviews would describe these forces as "magical" or "supernatural," in the sense of "pretend," or "figments of the imagination," in the Christian vision, they are no less real than other, separate forms of creation, like mammals, fish, and celestial bodies. In the Christian paradigm these beings are part of the ontological fabric of reality, impacting and influencing life on earth and the interactions of human beings. God, of course, is the ultimate being within this supernatural realm, the creator of all that is.[9]

Nor is the Christian God a deistic one, setting the world and the cosmos in motion, but remaining detached and set apart from his creation. As the Apostle Paul says to the Romans at the Areopagus, "in (God) we live and move and have our being."[10] This God not only creates, but sustains: holding the universe together, moment by moment. He is intensely active in his creation, acting and interacting within it, hearts beating and lungs breathing by the force of his sovereign will.

This perspective of God has implications on the Christian mind as it perceives such weighty subjects as identity, truth, nature, the universe, and meaning. From a Christian perspective, humans are externally referenced beings, created in the creator's image. This means their identity is defined by the nature and character of their creator, what that creator says about who they are, how they are made for each other, and how they are to interrelate and deal with one another.

Because the Christian perspective of God is one of immutability, human identity in the *imago Dei* is relatively fixed, not subject to change.[11] Truth, and what it means to be true, is also rooted in the nature and character, the very being of God. Therefore, like God, truth is absolute, fixed, immutable, not fully known, and in many cases, unknowable and subject to mystery.

Conversely, from a secular, naturalistic perspective, humans are primarily *self*-referenced beings. From the philosophical tradition of Descartes and Kant, modern Westerners perceive themselves as primarily individualized and autonomous; their identity is, in large part, characterized by what they say about themselves, and, as such, is subject to change. Because truth is also subject to individualized perception and is, in some sense, self-referenced, it is not nearly as absolute, fixed, and immutable as in the Christian way of thinking.

Given the Christian perspective that God is a sovereign God, who has the freedom to act and does act upon his creation at his election and will, Christians perceive creation as an open system. It is not, as the famous metaphor indicates, a watch. Or if it is, the watch still has its back removed, and the watchmaker is constantly turning the dials and gears.

A naturalistic perspective, that necessarily embraced in a public school context, is nature as closed system, subject to highly complex processes, reactions, and interactions that are, nevertheless, confined within the system itself. The box has no lid, and there is nothing outside the box. Rather than conceiving of the world and cosmos as "creation," it is "nature," which can be known and defined. [12]

This conceptual disparity of the nature of nature also has semiotic implications. From a naturalistic perspective, meaning exists within nature itself and has no transcendent dependence. Again, channeling Kant, human beings construct and attach meaning based upon their sensory perception of nature around them. Science sits on the epistemic throne of secular naturalism, because perceiving, measuring, drawing conclusions, and constructing meaning from nature is the very essence of modern science.

Christian meaning is found in revelation, God revealing truth to man, not only through the scriptures, but through his creation. Creation is pregnant with meaning, waiting to be revealed and discovered by human beings. Creation reveals truth about itself, its own nature and character. [13]

Revelation is progressive, meaning that humans know more about creation at this point in time than at any previous point, but less than they will tomorrow. The Christian concept of revelation also carries with it the idea of common grace insight, that God reveals truth about creation and life not only to those who believe in him, but also to those who reject his existence. [14]

While science and technology are important epistemic tools in the Christian paradigm, helping humans understand more about God's creation, they are not exclusive ways of knowing: creation also reveals deeper, transcendent truths about God's nature and character in the Christian way of thinking.

This is not to say that those who profess a Christian faith have not been profoundly impacted by Western culture over the past five hundred years, and are not creatures of reform and the Enlightenment. We are all, to one degree or another, secular, because we live in the current age. Nor is it to suggest that Christian education is about some sort of repristination movement, a pining for a return to Eden. The Christian idea of progressive revelation, that God is continually revealing his creation, militates against a philosophical retreat to some premodern halcyon era.

Yet Christian thought also strains against what C. S. Lewis called "chronological snobbery," the modern impulse to believe that the advance of science and technology renders us intellectually superior to our philosophical and theological forebears. [15] A Christian perspective argues for the "both/and"—taking those philosophical presuppositions of our ancestors, as improved upon or further nuanced or interpreted by subsequent revelation, and building one's vision of the good life upon all. [16]

EPISTEMIC SMACKDOWN

These conflicting visions of life and reality have epistemic ramifications on both curriculum and pedagogy in public and Christian schools. The basic view of Christian epistemology is predicated upon a divine sense of belief in God, and the internal testimony of the Holy Spirit, which underlies belief in the doctrines of Christianity. This belief transcends reason, because it does not originate in traditional elements of reason, such as memory, perception, intuition, or testimony.

Yet it does not follow that these beliefs are irrational or fanciful, despite the fact that they stand apart from science and reason. There are other, nonscientific ways of knowing that, along with religious faith, can also correct and be corrected by science and reason, including emotion, imagination, language, logic, ethics, and aesthetics. [17]

Yet while these other ways of knowing can be explored in public education, matters of faith, Christian or otherwise, are precluded from the public school context by a necessary predisposition to *methodical naturalism*—necessary because of public education's epistemic precommitment to secularism by modern conceptions of separation of church and state.

Methodical naturalism is the idea that neither data for scientific investigation nor a scientific theory can properly refer to supernatural beings, employ what one knows or thinks by divine revelation, or acknowledge that the probability or plausibility of a theory requires an epistemic base that requires the existence of God or other supernatural agents. [18]

This epistemic preclusion is perhaps most evident in the line of cases addressing the teaching of the various strains of creationism in the public schools. Whether known as creationism, creation science, or intelligent design, each of these initiatives was an historical attempt by people of faith, mostly Christians, to integrate faith and science as coexistent epistemic constructs within the American public school system.

First with the U.S. Supreme Court in *Epperson v. Arkansas* (1968), then *Edwards v. Aguillard* (1987), then with lower courts in cases such as *Kitz-*

miller v. Dover Area School District (2005), wherever these initiatives were challenged in the courts, they were rejected. In each of these cases, the introduction of the idea, concept, or curriculum allowing for the possibility of supernatural influence in the origin of life discussions in the public schools under review were defined by their opponents, and acknowledged by the courts, as religious in nature and, therefore, excluded under the First Amendment Establishment Clause.

The point is not that these cases were incorrectly decided; given the current state of American jurisprudence and the public school system, the courts ruled correctly. But neither Christians, nor Christian schools (as, presumably, other religious private schools) must subject themselves to the same epistemic barriers as does the unitary state public school system.

Not subscribing to those impediments allows for a much more philosophically robust education, the ability for teachers and students to explore truth in all its forms, and for students to ultimately exercise their God-given free will to come to their own conclusions, rather than being driven to certain conclusions by limited ways of knowing.

The ability to view all life and learning through an expanded lens encompassing a supernatural realm, an open system of creation, an externally referenced view of the self, and the idea of revelation and meaning inherent in the created order, all equate to distinctively different ways of viewing the Christian school's entire curriculum and pedagogy: not only science and technology, but politics, history, language, government, sociology, and all aspects of human inquiry.[19]

Beliefs also influence action, and a broader Christian school epistemology impacts not only curriculum and pedagogy, but has a dramatic impact upon how Christian schools view every aspect of their school cultures. Christian beliefs and philosophy impact school leadership, governance, and training, professional development, community dynamics, school approaches to student discipline, personnel policies and preparation, and everything that makes up the ecology of a school community.

To suggest that public school education and Christian or other religious education can be substantially equivalent because both teach English and math is to say that a Subaru and the space shuttle are substantially equivalent vehicles because both have tires and windows. One is dramatically different from the other; "substantial equivalency" is a term without meaning in this case, and religious school families choose religious schooling for the very reason that they do not *want* a substantially equivalent education for their children.

Christian and other religious schools are not legally required to philosophically hem themselves in, and are free to expand their philosophical bases to embrace a broader epistemology than their secular, public counterparts. For Christian and other religious private schools to be forced to realign themselves epistemically in order to achieve "substantial equivalency" with public schools, as interpreted by that same hemmed-in state, would fundamentally alter both the nature of religious schools themselves and the religious tenets that support them.

In time, religious schools run the risk of becoming like the unitary state schools: epistemically homogeneous, but sheathed in a veneer of religiosity, and neutered of their transformational power. It is this type of freedom of conscience the First Amendment Free Exercise Clause was designed to protect.

A BETTER WAY

There is no doubt that the state has a right and an expectation to ensure a well-educated citizenry; indeed, it is a public trust. Far from promoting an educated citizenry, however, the process of epistemic homogenization inherent in schemes like New York's "substantial equivalency" regulations actually undermine the very common good they seek to achieve.

America is not Japan or Finland; her genius lay not in her homogeneity, but in her diversity: in different, well-educated voices speaking cogently into the marketplace of ideas. The state subverts its own self-interest in diversity when it attempts to homogenize. Highlighted elsewhere in this volume, Ashley Berner advocates for educational pluralism (allowing public funds to follow children to their family's choice of K–12 school, including religious schools), in order to promote this very diversity.[20] Charles Glenn argues state homogenization is a type of state establishment in its own right, subject to constitutional issues.[21]

Whether American K–12 educational pluralism is funded by the state, private entities, or parents, it is a public good for the very reason it provides, on the whole, well-educated voices speaking philosophically-diverse messages into the landscape of ideas and perspectives, stronger theses and antitheses generating more powerful national syntheses.

Citizens educated in Christian schools and other private schools are as likely as those educated in public schools to seek the welfare of their local and broader communities, promoting the common good. Research by Cardus, studying alumni from public and private sectarian and nonsectarian schools throughout North America over nearly a decade, revealed that public and private school students receive very similar training in civic engagement during their K–12 experiences.

Furthermore, public and private school alumni have strikingly similar interests and engagement in the political process, involvement in their local communities, support of free speech, participation in working to eliminate injustice, and other measures of civic engagement. This, despite the findings

that Christian school graduates in particular are also more likely to participate in their local congregations and give to charities, over and above their
civic engagement and involvement.[22]

Educational diversity not only promotes a greater wealth in viewpoints,
but also promotes innovation in education. Nearly half of private, independent schools are organized around unique pedagogical features. Innovation at
these levels can contribute to greater innovation at the public level.[23]

States that are so inclined can ensure private schools within their jurisdictions meet standards for high academic quality by requiring that those
schools be accredited, and compelling accrediting bodies to follow broad
standards of best practices contributing to excellence in education. States
may require only graduates from recognized, accredited schools to apply and
enroll in state colleges and universities, and even private colleges and universities that receive state funding.

Strong accreditation practices help ensure that students are educated in
schools committed to principles of continuous improvement, all the while
recognizing those schools' distinct educational missions and operational independence that actually undergird and contribute to strong national and
local interests.

"Substantially equivalent" schools are not only an impossible standard,
but an undesirable one, given an American society that (at its best) prides
itself on diversity of thought, belief, and culture.

Developing a strong commitment to best practices and continuous improvement through accreditation that recognizes, respects, and appreciates
each school's missional uniqueness and religious and philosophical freedom,
while at the same time creating accountability to the continuous process of
becoming better at that mission than it once was, will help ensure the strongest thought, the noblest belief, and cultures that promote enduring images of
the good life, contributing to a clear vision for the common good.

NOTES

1. Henry J. Perkinson, *The Imperfect Panacea: American Faith in Education* (New York: McGraw-Hill, Inc., 1995).

2. Robert N. Bellah, "Civil Religion in America," *Journal of the American Academy of Arts and Sciences* 96, no. 1 (1967): 1–21.

3. Engel v. Vitale, 370 U.S. 421 (1962).

4. School District of Abington Township v. Schempp, 374 U.S. 203 (1963).

5. Courts have routinely held that the Bible, Torah, Koran, and other religious texts can be reviewed in a public school curriculum for their literary value. Courts have further held that comparative religion curriculum is acceptable as well, as a way of learning about religion in public schools (School District of Abington Township v. Schempp 1963). Presumably driven by fear of litigation, or that Bible curriculum will be used for proselytizing, such curriculum is the rare exception, rather than the rule, in the public school context.

6. James K. A. Smith, *Desiring the Kingdom: Worship, Worldview, and Culture Formation* (Grand Rapids: Baker Academic, 2009).

7. The Association of Christian Schools International, Christian Schools International, and other Christian school accrediting bodies require that educators new to Christian education within their schools engage in fairly extensive training and reading in what constitutes a Christian philosophy of education. Even so, at the higher education level, many teacher-training programs at colleges and universities with a distinctively-Christian mission do not, as a part of their teacher training, instill their teachers with such a philosophy. This is so, in large part, because many of those departments are led by former public school administrators who are followers of Jesus, but did not themselves have any such philosophical training.

8. Charles Taylor, *A Secular Age* (Cambridge: The Belknap Press of Harvard University Press, 2007).

9. Many of these concepts are Christian only in the sense that they are part of what Christians call "the New Covenant," as revealed in the New Testament. They have their roots in the Old Testament, the Hebrew Bible, and hence are actually Hebraic in origin.

10. Acts 17:28.

11. Ted Peters, "Imago Dei, DNA, and the Transhuman Way," *Theology and Science* 16 (2018).

12. Terence L. Nichols, *The Sacred Cosmos: Christian Faith and the Challenge of Naturalism* (Eugene: Wipf & Stock, 2003).

13. Richard A. Riesen, *Piety and Philosophy* (Phoenix: ACW Press, 2002).

14. Albert M. Wolters, *Creation Regained: Biblical Basics for a Reformational Worldview* (Grand Rapids: Wm. B. Eerdmans Publishing Co., 2005).

15. C. S. Lewis, *Surprised by Joy* (New York: HarperCollins, 1955).

16. Rich Nathan and Insoo Kim, *Both-And: Living in the Christ-Centered Life of an Either-Or World* (Downers Grove: InterVarsity Press, 2013).

17. Alvin Plantiaga, "Religion and Science," in *The Stanford Encyclopedia of Philosophy* (Stanford: Stanford University, 2012).

18. J. P. Moreland and William Lane Craig, *Philosophical Foundations for a Christian Worldview*, second edition (Downers Grove: InterVarsity Press, 2017).

19. Pew Research Center, "America's Changing Religious Landscape," research report (Washington, DC: Pew Research Center, 2015), https://www.pewforum.org/2015/05/12/americas-changing-religious-landscape/. The idea of privatization of one's faith so common in legal discourse—that religious belief is a private affair and should not play a role in public life—is really only possible if one's faith is deism. If one actually believes in a sovereign God who created and speaks into every field of human and supernatural endeavor, then privatizing God is impossible unless religious people choose to withdraw from the marketplace of ideas altogether, or ignore whatever they believe God would have them think or do about all of life and learning. Neither is palatable or advisable, given that nearly 80 percent of Americans claim some belief in God.

20. Ashley Berner, "The Case for Educational Pluralism in the U.S.," report (New York: Manhattan Institute for Policy Research, 2019), https://www.manhattan-institute.org/educational-pluralism-in-united-states.

21. Charles L. Glenn, "Disestablishing Our Secular Schools," *First Things*, January 2012, https://www.firstthings.com/article/2012/01/disestablishing-our-secular-schools.

22. Cardus, "Private Schools for the Public Good," research report (Hamilton: Cardus Education Survey, 2014).

23. Ray Pennings, "Independent Schools Contribute to the Public Good and Deserve Public Support," *The Star*, August 12, 2019, https://www.thestar.com/opinion/contributors/2019/08/12/independent-schools-contribute-to-the-public-good-and-deserve-public-support.html.

Chapter Nine

Between Tradition and Regulation

What Can Muslim Education Offer the West?

Jibran Khan

The great Yale scholar of the Near East, Franz Rosenthal, who is most famous for his magisterial translation of Ibn Khaldūn's *Muqaddimah*, described knowledge as the foundation of Muslim civilization, so much so that he devoted his greatest original work, *Knowledge Triumphant*, to the topic.

In it, he writes that "there is no other concept that has been operative as a determinant of Muslim civilization in all its aspects to the same extent as *'ilm* [knowledge]. There is no branch of Muslim intellectual life, of Muslim religious and political life, and of the daily life of the average Muslim that remained untouched by the all-pervasive attitude toward 'knowledge' as something of supreme value for Muslim being."[1]

To illustrate by contrast, Muslims refer to the culture of the pagan Arabs before Islam as the age of ignorance (*jāhiliyyah*). Even at the level of basic descriptive language, Islam traditionally associates itself with education. This is rooted in Islam's metaphysics, for the Qur'an holds that "God taught Adam all of the names."[2] And this revealed knowledge was passed down, to be approached properly. Truth proceeds from *wahi* (revelation). Abuse of learning was concerned sinful, as was covetousness of knowledge.

The jurist Adh-Dhahabī believed that gaining knowledge came with the obligation to pass this knowledge on to others who are deserving of learning, comparing the obligation of teaching to the obligation to give in charity. "Such a tax is even more necessary in the case of knowledge," he argued, "as knowledge is increased by spending."[3] This makes it clear not only that knowledge is definitional to Islam, but that education is baked in as an imperative.

The fact that this tradition of learning has survived to the present day, taking on different cultural complexions yet still recognizably similar, is important. It did so in the almost complete absence of state involvement—a more recent phenomenon that has already heavily damaged traditional learning. The continuity itself is significant, but even more so is the way in which it was transmitted through a variety of cultures, many of which had no historic link to the Semitic soil in which Islam was born.

EDUCATION IN ISLAM

The Muslims were able to do this because, from the beginning, their approach to education was grounded first in acquiring a methodology for study. As Shaykh Hamza Yusuf, president and founder of Zaytuna College, put it, "Arabic rhetoric develops in Central Asia and is added to grammar and logic in a triad of subjects, foundational to the Islamic tradition, that become known as the instrumental arts (*al-'ulūm al-ālah*) and sometimes as the three arts (*al-sinā'āt al-thalāth*). Thus, the trivium becomes fully incorporated into Muslim scholastic tradition. Grammar, however, remains the focus."[4]

As Islam spread to Central Asia, Persia, and Syria, which had their own traditions of learning, including Buddhist logic and Hellenic philosophy, it was these non-Arabs who analyzed and systematized the grammar and rhetoric of Arabic, which had been unnecessary for the Arabs, for whom it was their native tongue and whose tradition was mostly oral. This was critical, for it was the vessel of Divine Speech.[5] The linking of these regions by a common language of scholarship opened the way to the exchange of ideas, and for the expression of the same Muslim theology in different technical languages.

This Arabic-speaking tradition[6] of learning, according to the late historian George Makdisi in his *The Rise of Colleges: Institutions of Learning in Islam and the West*, was heavily borrowed from by the Latin West. Furthermore, the common use of Arabic meant that a Moroccan jurist (Ibn Battuta) could serve as a judge on the far-flung Maldive Islands of the Indian Ocean or a Spanish rabbi (*Musa ibn Maymun*, or Maimonides) could serve as a physician in Egypt.

Islam is a religion of law (*shari'ah*), encompassing both acts of worship (*'ibādāt*) and interpersonal transactions (*mu'āmalāt*). Because of this conception, the Shari'ah categorized the training of jurists—as well as their room, board, and travel—as a "communal obligation" (*fard kifayah*), meaning that, were it to be absent in any given locale, the Muslims of that area would incur collective sin.[7]

Furthermore, every individual Muslim is required to learn his or her individual Shari'ah obligations (*fard 'ayn*), which by necessity requires qualified instructors. In the realm of jurisprudence (*fiqh*), once again the

Muslim tradition turns to developing the tools of study first. Muslims looked at the same scriptural sources, the Qur'ān and Sunnah, but came to different conclusions.

> Shafi'i's system of minimising mistakes in the derivation of Islamic rulings from the mass of evidence came to be known as *usul al-fiqh* (the roots of *fiqh*). . . . In time, each of the great interpretative traditions of Sunni Islam codified its own variation on these roots, thereby yielding in some cases divergent branches (i.e., specific rulings on practice). Although the debates generated by these divergences could sometimes be energetic, nonetheless, they were insignificant when compared to the great sectarian and legal disagreements which had arisen during the first two centuries of Islam before the science of *usul al-fiqh* had put a stop to such chaotic discord.[8]

Each interpretative tradition (*madhhab*) has its own methodology, which is considered an extension of the science of logic. Today, it is difficult to conceive of a culture in which matters of law themselves are subject to differences of opinion, both inter- and intra-*madhhab*, let alone one in which these differences were all considered legitimate. A decentralized society, with law generated by non-state actors and enforced by independent judges and lawyers, was seen as a feature, not a bug.

Malik ibn Anas, founder of one of the four major legal traditions in Islam, compiled the *Muwatta*, an early collection of oral tradition and legal rulings that remains one of Islam's most reliable sources of narrations attributed to the Prophet. Biographical accounts note that Malik was approached by then-caliph al-Mansur, who stated that he wished to make the *Muwatta* the standard legal code throughout the Abbasid Empire (which then spanned from parts of India, the whole of Persia, Syria, and the Arabian peninsula, to North Africa).[9]

Malik refused, saying that this would cause harm, because it would impose a singular interpretation of the Law, even if it was one that he himself supported, on people who had legitimately come to different yet equally acceptable opinions. This speaks to the polycentric nature of Islam's Sacred Law.

AMERICAN MUSLIM INSTITUTIONS OF LEARNING

Given the critical nature of education to Islam, and the fact that interpretive diversity is an integral part of it, it will come as no surprise that Muslim education in the United States does not follow a single model. Broadly, these consist of three types of institutions.

First are the Muslim schools, which like most confessional schools in America are essentially private schools that focus on a secular curriculum with a small Islam or Arabic component. The second is the traditional Muslim seminary (madrasa), which can be regarded as the most direct application of traditional Muslim pedagogy in America, focusing on developing instrumental skills and knowledge of the religious sciences. The third, and newest, model is the Muslim college, which is a hybrid of the American liberal arts college and a traditional madrasa.

Given their structure, typical Muslim schools in America would *seem* less likely to be affected much by a "substantial equivalency" standard—however, this depends on the interpretation of the "substantial equivalence," which may even object to the religious supplement.

In the United Kingdom, the situation has been different due to diktats from the ruling Conservative government, which demands that private schools teach what they call a "British values" curriculum. Because some of this material contradicts Muslim, Jewish, and traditional Christian moral teaching, high-performing schools, primarily Muslim and Jewish, have faced crackdowns from state authorities that threaten to shut them down. [10]

It is difficult to imagine such legislation being passed at the national level in the United States, and should a local or state jurisdiction attempt to do so, it is likely to face a legal challenge on religious liberty grounds. Still, legal norms are built on cultural norms, and as such, the debate in Britain is not irrelevant to the discourse in the United States. The standoff among parents, schools, regulators, and the state in Britain calls for close observation.

TRADITIONAL PEDAGOGY

The traditional madrasa is found throughout the Muslim world, with regional variations. At a madrasa, whether a student is training for Quranic memorization or in the religious sciences, the core learning principles are constantly reemphasized. These are articulated in a practice of "repetition, review, and accuracy" in the words of the young American scholar Omar Popal of the Tanwir Institute.

Popal took a break from traditional high school education after ninth grade to study at a madrasa in South Africa. His madrasa teachers so emphasized the importance of education that they inspired him to make an early return to the United States, where he would study in a madrasa environment while also engaging in a rigorous homeschool curriculum.

Where before his break, he had been an average student, not particularly engaged in school, he found that this had changed dramatically after his exposure to the traditional Muslim pedagogy. "These are classical curricula," he says, "built on patience and discipline. And their intended objective is to *build a student*, not to create scholars."

By this, he refers to the traditional emphasis on the tools of learning, which extend well beyond the classroom and are meant to adapt themselves to new situations throughout the student's life. Popal found himself naturally applying the practices he had learned in that environment to his secular studies, breaking down each book and ensuring that he had understood each section accurately, on both thematic and language grounds.

Because of this, he moved quickly through the social science and humanities books in his homeschooling program. He needed to work on his mathematics, however. Since his new analytical skills allowed him to work through the other material so efficiently, this meant he could dedicate more time to it, and quickly caught up with the help of his madrasa teachers and online resources like Khan Academy. Traditional education so improved his ability to learn, he says he wishes he had taken it on for all twelve years of school, rather than just the last three.

Asked about the prospect of requirements that would dictate time allocation for students, Popal saw this not so much as forcing in new material but as limiting the potential of study. As he puts it, "If you limit a child's exposure to a subject, they won't know if they have a knack for it or not." Arabic grammar, for example, needs ample time to study properly. (The contrast in Arabic skills between the average madrasa student and the university Arabic student speaks to this.) Furthermore, grammar in the context of Arabic is a broader field than generally imagined.

As Shaykh Hamza Yusuf puts it: "Jonathan Owens cogently argues that the grammarians of Islam were closer to what we would today call *linguists*. They studied every aspect of language, including deeply philosophical problems related to language."[11] A student will not necessarily be using Arabic grammar to do, say, English homework, but skills cross-pollinate. Popal explains that his Arabic studies prepared him to immediately analyze every part of a sentence and look at exactly what each component is doing. He found himself getting much more out of literature, at which he came to excel due to this training.

In fact, the madrasa system of instruction is so effective at building learners that it has spawned a fascinating social-welfare organization, the Tayba Foundation. Prisoners who pursue postsecondary education while incarcerated are half as likely to recidivate. Tayba, founded by Rami Nsour, an American Muslim scholar who studied Islam in Mauritania, has developed a curriculum spanning from the core skills of learning and etiquette to the Arabic language and Quranic recitation to history to advanced training in law and theology.

Tayba supplies books that include both the Arabic source texts and English translations, encouraging students to begin memorizing and learning the Arabic from the very beginning. Students complete exams, write essays, and, when they are ready, have the opportunity to receive traditional licensure (*ijāzah*), which is the indication that someone has learned a book well enough to transmit it, with a chain (*sanad*) that goes back to the author.

Because this approach to learning is holistic and takes an individual rather than a one-size-fits-all approach, Tayba also works on building good character, addressing criminality, and teaching parenting and family skills. Using the tools of traditional Muslim learning, the teachers at Tayba are helping to reform and develop strong individuals who can be productive members of society.

Current students, both male and female, number in the thousands, distributed in prisons throughout the country. While prisons do not generally fall under the purview of education regulators, many state departments of corrections and prison wardens place strong restrictions on what materials prisoners are allowed to read. Tayba's success in the harshest of conditions speaks to how traditional Muslim pedagogy caters to areas of learning that mainstream education does not. It should be hoped that prison regulations do not get in the way of this project, which shares its purported aim of rehabilitation.

The madrasa system that is best represented in the United States (as well as in the United Kingdom) is the Indian model, which follows the *Dars-e-Nizami* curriculum. A nineteenth-century British description (included in the first issue of *The Atlantic*) details how it compares to Western education:

> Perhaps there are few communities in the world, among whom education is more generally diffused than among Mahomedans in India. He who holds an office worth twenty rupees a month, commonly gives his sons an education equal to that of a prime minister. They learn, through the medium of the Arabic and Persian languages, what young men in our colleges learn through those of the Greek and Latin—that is, grammar, rhetoric, and logic. After his seven years of study, the young Mahomedan binds his turban upon a head almost as well filled with the things which appertain to these three branches of knowledge, as the young man raw from Oxford—he will talk as fluently about Socrates and Aristotle, Plato and Hippocrates, Galen and Avicenna, *alias* Socrate, Aristotalees, Aflaton, Bocrate, Jaleenoos, and Booalee Sehna. . . .
>
> On the faculties and operations of the human mind on man's passions and affections, and his duties in all relations of life, the works of Imam Mahomed Ghuzallee and Nirseerooddeen Jansee, hardly yield to those of Plato and Aristotle, or to those of any other authors who have ever written on the same subjects in any country. These works . . . are the great 'Pierian spring' of moral instruction, from which the Mahomedan delights to 'drink deep' from infancy to old age, and a better spring it would be difficult to find in the works of any other. [12]

Today it entails a foundation year of Arabic language teaching, so that the student is able to directly access the texts in their original form, alongside basic theology and law, and analytical skills. [13] This is then followed by four to six years of full-time instruction in the religious sciences like jurisprudence and spirituality, which assume basic Arabic fluency (and continue to develop it with advanced instruction in grammar and rhetoric, which are considered lifetime pursuits). Students also study history, English literature, and other "secular" subjects, because these contribute to a well-rounded understanding.

As the madrasas of old, integrated, indigenous intellectual cultures, the American madrasa is an American institution and seeks to contribute to learning on those terms. Darul Qasim in Chicago is engaged deeply in bio-ethics projects with the University of Chicago. As part of this, the scholars at Darul Qasim have sifted through 1,400 years of Islam's literary tradition, to find ethical discussions that are analogous to, or in some cases directly match, discussions that are relevant today.

Darul Qasim's programs are roughly analogous to a BA, MA, and so on for easy reference, with intense academic rigor. (This is not a uniquely American phenomenon; many of the great centers of learning in the Muslim world operate on a private basis, mutually recognizing their credentials as a non-state standard, following the Indian scholar Mawlana Ashraf Ali Thanvi's principle of *istighnā*, independence from state funding and oversight. This principle has ensured academic freedom in South Asian madrasas not enjoyed in the modern Middle East.)

Despite this, it has built a reputation for strong academic work, evidenced by its strong links to both the medical and oriental studies programs at University of Chicago.

Zaytuna College in Berkeley, California, was founded by Shaykh Hamza Yusuf and Imam Zaid Shakir, two of the most prominent American Muslim scholars. It is so far the first of its kind in the United States.

In England, Cambridge University professor Timothy Winter, also known as Abdal Hakim Murad, has founded the Cambridge Muslim College, which is a similar project and relevant to the present discussion due to the Anglophone environment present in both countries. Each integrates the pedagogy of traditional Islam with the Anglo-American intellectual tradition, but to slightly different ends. Describing their approach, Shaykh Hamza writes,

> At Zaytuna College, we have set out to do our best at restoring the broad-based, holistic tradition of what in the West was called the liberal arts, and in the Muslim civilization was known as comprehensive studies (*al-dirāsāt al-jāmiʿah*), which lead one to become an *adīb*, which approximates the English concept of the erudite gentleman.

> The ancients understood the world not as matter without purpose but through the matrix of four causes—material, efficient, formal, and final—that placed purpose at the highest level of inquiry. This is the lens through which we can view Muslim efforts to help restore this lost tradition, begin-

ning with the final cause, which answers the question "What is the purpose of education?" The purpose of education from an Islamic perspective—and for Zaytuna College—is to aid students in their own pursuit and discovery of the truth. The Islamic epistemological framework remains rooted in the three laws of thought: the law of identity, the law of the excluded middle, and the law of non-contradiction. Students learn this early on. [14]

Zaytuna seeks to embody the ideal of an American liberal arts college, built around a strong core of Muslim pedagogy and the study of Muslim sciences. Most American liberal arts colleges were founded by some denomination or other, after all, but for the most part, that aspect has been reduced to little more than a historical detail. In a sense, the Zaytuna project is to revive a neglected *American* tradition, the denominational liberal arts college, with a Muslim ethos.

Whereas madrasas usually focus on a single *madhhab* of law, Zaytuna undergraduates choose which one they will study, in recognition of the various ethnic and cultural backgrounds in American Islam. [15] Zaytuna students have been highly successful in their pursuit of postgraduate studies, including in scientific fields due to an arrangement with the University of California, Berkeley, which allows Zaytuna students to take science courses there.

In order to retain an independent character, Zaytuna refuses government funding, relying instead on donations from across the American Muslim community. So successful have they been at cultivating a ground-up funding model, itself part of the Muslim tradition, that they are now able to cover all tuition and housing costs for undergraduates and graduates alike.

Cambridge Muslim College, in contrast, features a more madrasa-like curriculum, focused on a deep study of the Muslim sciences, combined with strong engagement with the history and culture of Britain. It is part of a broader project of Anglo-Muslim culture that Dr. Winter has been engaged in for decades. Like Zaytuna, Cambridge Muslim College is accredited, but it is unique in that it accepts a small batch of students every three years. Each class moves together through the full curriculum.

Both approaches are suited to the countries in which they are based, and it will be interesting to see how they serve as models for future institutions. As postsecondary institutions, they are not subject to the same type of educational regulation as schools, but they do not exist in a vacuum. After all, they are best suited to students who have a basis of training before they enter college, and should the regulatory environment make that difficult, it will hurt the potential of these institutions to attract the best Muslim students in the West.

There has been a revival of Great Books approaches to education, and a whole movement inspired by novelist Dorothy L. Sayers's essay *The Lost Tools of Learning*. The presence and competition of educational philosophies, whether Sayers's *trivium* revival, Waldorf education, or the principles of Kurt Hahn, are healthy for education. The Muslim tradition of learning, though, has a particular edge.

With the nature of direct teacher-to-student transmission, the widely distributed educational traditions of Islam, and the religious requirement for qualified scholarship, Muslim education forms a continuous tradition going back to the earliest days of the religion, and integrating philosophies that are even older.

It is undeniable that Muslim education does not have quite the prominence that it did in the famed medieval "Golden Age," and that the authoritarian turn of governments within the Muslim world has brought state repression and control to religious education, which would have been considered unthinkable in premodern times. Morocco now has civil servants dictating the curricula of madrasas!

While the American tradition of intellectual freedom remains robust enough that this has not happened, such examples should serve as a caution all the same. The repression of Muslim education opens the door to autodidacts, lacking any instrumental skills and grounding. This unmoored approach has been a major contributor to extremism and violence, allowing for violent and intolerant opinions that go against the (traditionally binding) consensus of orthodox jurists.

Ashley Berner and Charles Glenn, citing new research from the University of Virginia, note that American Muslim schools produce graduates with strong civil values, well-inoculated against the propaganda of radicalism.[16]

It should come as no surprise that violent groups place religious scholars at the top of their kill lists, for these are the people that expose them as the brutal frauds that they are. The solution to this is to allow traditional Muslim education, a challenge to such claimants on first principles, to flourish. Here, global comparisons provide strong examples. Westerners educated in madrasas were strongly resistant to radicalization. Countries like India, where the madrasas are strongly independent, produce far fewer radicals than those with state-run religious institutions.[17]

Despite repression by state actors, because individual scholarship is so diffused (*tawatur*), the tradition remains alive and thriving. It has the potential to link American students to a chain (*sanad*) going back to the Classics, providing an alternative paradigm that is nonetheless intimately related to the rest of Abrahamic civilization. Dr. Winter argues,

> As instability grows in the Middle East and curricula are subject to regime encroachment, it is likely that our *majnun* (lover [of knowledge]) will consider this option [the study of Islam in the West] more seriously than he might have done 20 years ago. It entails, for a Western Muslim, a kind of *hijra* (migration) within, not to faraway *madrasas* in a ruined *Dar al-Islam* (Muslim countries) but to a different habitat where freedoms are more actual and, in fact, claim to

be zealously guarded. . . . Could it be that a *hijra* **from**, rather than to, the *Dar al-Islam* and its wrecked institutions is now to be advised?

Much as the Muslim scholastics influenced the development of their Latin counterparts in the Middle Ages, Muslim education in the United States, where it has the protection of religious and intellectual liberty, will flourish and contribute to the broader educational culture. At least, this is so long as these liberties are actually present and not rendered impotent by regulators.

NOTES

1. Franz Rosenthal, *Knowledge Triumphant: The Concept of Knowledge in Medieval Islam*, Brill Classics in Islam, vol. 2 (Boston; Leiden: Brill, 2006), 2.

2. Qur'an 2:31.

3. Franz Rosenthal, "Materials for an Appraisal of Knowledge as a Societal Force," in *Man Versus Society in Medieval Islam*, ed. Dimitri Gutas, Brill Classics in Islam, vol. 7 (Boston; Leiden: Brill, 2014), 983.

4. Hamza Yusuf Hanson, "Medina and Athena: Restoring a Lost Legacy," *Renovatio: The Journal of Zaytuna College* 3, no. 1 (Spring 2019), https://renovatio.zaytuna.edu/article/medina-and-athena-restoring-a-lost-legacy.

5. Due to this nature, the Qur'an is the supreme epistemological source for Muslims, making the study of its language a shared building block across myriad cultures' education.

6. The use of "Arabic-speaking" here is deliberate, as this educational culture was not solely Muslim. Bernard Lewis notes in *The Jews of Islam* (Princeton: Princeton University Press, 1987) that it included a thriving, parallel system of Jewish learning, of which Maimonides is the most famous example. As Judaism and Islam alike are staunchly unitarian and emphasize the Law, many foundational works cross-pollinated and a shared vocabulary developed.

7. Obligations in Islam are separated into individual obligations (*fard al-ayn*) and communal obligations (*fard al-kifayah*). Every individual Muslim is required to learn and practice his or her basic acts of worship. In contrast, for communal obligations, it suffices for the practice or role to be established in the community, whether that is for religious jurists or doctors or any other such role.

8. Timothy (Abdal Hakim Murad) Winter, *Understanding the Four Madhhabs: The Facts about Ijtihad and Taqlid* (London: Muslim Academic Trust, 2009), http://masud.co.uk/understanding-the-four-madhhabs-the-problem-with-anti-madhhabism/.

9. Umar F. Abd-Allah, *Mālik and Medina: Islamic Legal Reasoning in the Formative Period*, Islamic History and Civilization 101 (Leiden: Brill, 2013), 57–58.

10. Jibran Khan, "Amanda Spielman's War on Religion in Great Britain," *National Review Online*, January 28, 2019, https://www.nationalreview.com/2019/01/amanda-spielman-religious-schools-england-secularism/.

11. Hanson, "Medina and Athena: Restoring a Lost Legacy."

12. William Henry Sleeman, *Rambles and Recollections of an Indian Official*, vol. 2 (London: Hatchard, 1844), 283–84.

13. So effective is this year that Darul Qasim, which was founded by the acclaimed scholar Shaykh Muhammad Amin Kholwadia, has in fact spun it off into a self-contained program in its own right. This allows both those who intend to pursue a full madrasa education and those who wish to pursue other fields to benefit from learning this formative learning apparatus first. It has also spawned a weekend program for otherwise full-time high school juniors and seniors, which is focused on teaching analytical skills, acts of worship, theology and logic, and the Prophetic tradition, so that they have a strong grasp on learning skills, to take with them to whichever further studies they hope to engage in.

14. Hanson, "Medina and Athena: Restoring a Lost Legacy."

15. While all of the schools are considered valid, one's *madhhab* is generally determined by geography, as one predominates in each region. Some historic centers of learning such as Syria and Egypt retain strong scholarship of all four.

16. Charles L. Glenn and Ashley Berner, "America's Muslim Schools and the Common Good," *The 74*, January 23, 2017, https://www.the74million.org/article/ashley-berner-and-charles-l-glenn-americas-muslim-schools-and-the-common-good/.

17. M. Danish Shakeel and Patrick J. Wolf, "Does Private Islamic Schooling Promote Terrorism? An Analysis of the Educational Background of Successful American Homegrown Terrorists," *Hungarian Educational Research Journal* 8, no. 1 (2018); Robert Maranto and M. Danish Shakeel, "Educating Believers: Lessons from School Choice Research," *Journal of School Choice* 12, no. 4 (2018), https://doi.org/10.1080/15582159.2018.1524412.

Chapter Ten

An Impossible (and Impermissible) Dream

Substantial Equivalency in Homeschools

Michael Donnelly

The response by the New York school authorities to accusations that certain yeshivas fail to provide a substantially equivalent education has been to create a highly intrusive set of regulations that would impair the schools' ability to carry out their mission to preserve Jewish culture and traditions.

When challenged by parents regarding his attempts to assert total state control over children through education in 1938 Germany, Adolf Hitler is reported to have said, "What are you? You will pass on. Your descendants, however, now stand in the new camp. In a short time, they will know nothing else but this new community."[1] Not very long after the Allied victory, a fledgling United Nations gathered to create a Universal Declaration on Human Rights (UDHR). In response to Germany's behavior, the United Nations declaration made two important statements regarding the parental role in education.

First in Article 23.6 the UDHR recognizes that "parents have a prior right to decide the kind of education" their children shall receive. And in article 16.3 it asserts that the family is the "fundamental group unit of society" entitled to protection by the state. In subsequent major human rights treaties, states took on binding international legal obligations to respect the rights of parents to ensure that the education of their children is in accordance with their philosophical and religious convictions.

At the core of the society-shaping struggle for control over education is a fundamental question of power. What power should determine the emotional, intellectual, and spiritual direction of children: parental or state? In this chapter I will explore this issue in the context of the modern home education movement.

In a way that no question about a brick-and-mortar school can, the modern homeschooling movement places all of these issues in focus. The consequences of allowing increased state control over home education or, synonymously, homeschooling, by demanding an "equivalent" education is fraught with philosophical, legal, and practical problems. It is an impossible task that should not be attempted in a free society where children ought to be under the primary influence of their parents.

A society that mandates the state to have the primary role in educating children or imposes strict controls on the right of parents to homeschool borders on tyranny.

HOMESCHOOLING CONTEXT

The growth of modern American homeschooling from essentially zero to now about 4 percent of the school-age population over the last 60 years is significant.[2] No other country in the world has anywhere remotely close to these numbers; it is even possible that all the other homeschooled children in the world would not total the number of homeschooled children in the United States.[3] The success of the movement in overcoming regulatory, legal, and cultural obstacles is a testament to the hard work and commitment of millions of parents and supporting organizations.

As much a social movement as an alternative educational modality, parents from the political left and right initiated the homeschooling movement in the late 1960s and 1970s. 1960s "progressives" responded to John Holt's anti-institutional message that schooling was not education while 1970s evangelicals responded to a growing and Supreme Court–driven secularization of public education by trying out homeschooling. By 1980 the movement had gained mass-media interest in both religious (James Dobson) and popular (Phil Donahue) media outlets.

The movement took off and grew rapidly, primarily among religious adherents who revealed, when asked by the U.S. government, that their most important reason for homeschooling was to provide religious or moral instruction to their children.[4] Although a majority of homeschooling parents continue to profess some religious motivation, this has become a secondary motivation to concerns about the environment in schools as shown by a comparison of the 2007 and 2012 NCES survey data.[5]

General educational research indicates that some of the most significant contributing factors to academic achievement in *all* learning environments are the amount of individual academic engagement by the student, parental involvement, and student motivation.[6] The hallmark of home education is high levels of all three factors coupled with an inherent capacity to innovate and flex to deliver an educational experience that is more customized to the individual needs, interests, and capacities of both children and parents.

In contrast, the bureaucratic requirements of public education deprive teachers and administrators of needed flexibility, constrain parental involvement, restrain individual creativity, and impose a one-size-fits-all approach to education that inhibits all of these contributing factors.

In the home environment, the teaching parent responds in real time to the learning needs of the child, catching errors and miscomprehension before they become entrenched. In homeschooling, student motivation is more internally driven and thus sustainable. In the home environment, the child engages in more active learning because there are fewer distractions than virtually any institutional environment.

By distraction I mean not only the classroom distractions that are the norm in public schools, such as classroom policing, peer-group drama, technology interruptions, and subject-matter disinterest, but also the "distractions" of having to use the same curriculum, to study the same subjects, and to learn in the same modality as everyone else. Since the late 1980s, thousands of research articles have been written about homeschooling with reports generally reporting positive outcomes for homeschooling in academic, social, and civic areas.[7]

However, the stakes can be very high for homeschooling families especially (but not only) in countries where its cultural acceptance is low and legal recognition is unclear.

HOMESCHOOLING CONTROVERSY

During the early years of homeschooling in the United States there was a significant amount of legislative, judicial, and executive action.[8] The activism of homeschooling parents was often confronted with opposition from teachers' unions and government education officials who expressed concern that children could and should only learn from "certified and trained teachers" in "brick and mortar" schools with expertly guided curriculum and scientifically developed assessments.[9]

The Home School Legal Defense Association's institutional experience over thirty-five years of homeschooling activism includes work representing homeschooling families relative to Child Protective Service (CPS) agencies, which often received referrals of "neglect" when children were not in school. This opposition as well as the real need for both legal and legislative protection and activism prompted the creation of civil society organizations in every state. By 1996 home education was explicitly recognized as legal in every state.

It is less common for families to be subject to investigations solely on account of homeschooling in the United States. In some countries homeschooling is viewed as a nefarious and neglectful activity resulting in prosecution for truancy or investigation of neglect with sometimes dramatic state intrusion into otherwise healthy, normal, and safe families. In some countries, children have been violently seized by authorities, families have been financially ruined, and parents sentenced to significant jail sentences.

In Germany and Sweden, Supreme Constitutional Courts have held that the state may prohibit the practice of homeschooling—especially (in the case of Germany) if it is motivated by religious or philosophical convictions. Since 1990, tens of thousands have been displaced from these countries who have chosen to flee rather than to face the harsh persecution by the state over their choice to homeschool.[10] Some families have even sought asylum protection in the United States on account of their fear over persecution because of their religious beliefs as well as their membership in a particular social group.

In a case of first impression in 2010, immigration judge Lawrence Burman granted asylum to a German family, the Romeikes, who had fled Germany in 2008 over harsh treatment because of their homeschooling. "I find that they belong to a particular social group of homeschoolers who, for some reason, the government chooses to treat as a rebel organization, a parallel society, for reasons of its own . . . this is Nazi doctrine, and it is, in this Court's mind, utterly repellant to everything that we believe in as Americans."[11]

Due to a lack of Jewish schools in Sweden, Rabbi Alexander and Leah Namdar had been homeschooling their children for decades. In June 2019 the Swedish Supreme Court upheld fines of $67,000 against them for violating the new anti-homeschooling statute, prompting international condemnation, particularly from Jewish groups.[12]

What could explain the state's motivation to prohibit homeschooling and treat families in such dramatic ways?

In 2003, in *Konrad*, Germany's Federal Constitutional Court held that the state could prohibit homeschooling by philosophically or religiously motivated parents because it had a "mandate" that was equal to that of the parents to ensure that children experienced "lived tolerance." The court held that these objectives would be more likely achieved by requiring children to attend an institutional government-approved school and that the German state had an equal interest in the education of children. The court reasoned that parents could not object to public education because it is supposed to be "neutral and secular."

The court also held that "the general public has an interest in counteracting the development of parallel societies and in integrating minorities." Because of this, the interference with the otherwise constitutionally recognized rights of parents was "reasonably commensurate" with the benefit to be expected from requiring that children attend school. Swedish authorities similarly rationalized their de facto prohibition on home education.

The *Wunderlich* case at the European Court of Human Rights (ECHR) involved four children who had been seized by German authorities solely over homeschooling. In January 2019, the court ruled that this act was within Germany's "margin of appreciation" with respect to its sovereign authority over education. [13]

In Norway in 2018, police chased and tackled a twelve-year-old boy who had been taken out of school to be homeschooled because he was being bullied at school.

In Cuba, a pastor and his wife and another father are in prison serving sentences ranging from one to three years for the "crime" of homeschooling. The independent lawyer who sought to assist them was beaten and sentenced to a year of hard labor.

In Kenya, parents and children were jailed for homeschooling.

In Brazil, a rapidly growing movement waits for federal legislation following the refusal of the Brazilian Supreme Court to grant clear constitutional recognition of homeschooling. [14]

The German FCC and the ECHR rulings do not meet international legal obligations. [15] Although a small group of academics agree with these courts, a 2014 study by Albert Cheng suggests that rather than foster intolerance, the more exposure a person had to homeschooling the more politically tolerant they were likely to be. [16]

Perhaps this should not be too surprising. As a minority, homeschoolers are more likely to appreciate the importance of protecting the rights of minorities. These findings could also suggest that children who are educated in a nurturing and affirming environment infused with love (such as the home)—and absent from the ethnic, class, and other divisions often present in institutional education—might be more willing to acknowledge the rights and inherent worth of others, despite their differences.

The ideological antipathy detailed above does not appear to have bled over into the mainstream of American policy making. Rather, the opposite has been the case in the past two decades as at least seventeen states have reduced government involvement in and oversight of homeschooling.

Ideological oversight appears absent entirely from the current state of regulation of homeschooling in the United States. Where states regulate home education explicitly (many do not), such oversight consists primarily of a limited set of criteria apparently designed to impose some modicum of equivalency, such as required subjects, teacher competency or credentials, required hours or days of attendance or instruction, and the requirement of some kind of method of assessing student progress (sometimes turned in to oversight authorities, sometimes not).

EQUIVALENCE—AN IMPOSSIBLE DREAM

It isn't difficult to understand why the framework of equivalence would be applied to home education initially. Generations of majorities (including judges, state legislators, and regulators) were educated through government-run schools and had virtually no other frame of reference.

Common curricular standards, teacher training and certification, and increased use of assessments to measure outcomes were ideas that most people associated with education. Applying these to the "novel" idea of home-schooling seems to make sense.

The idea that "just any old mom (or dad)" could educate a child to the same level as trained teachers using scientific standards, in government school buildings, informed by carefully constructed and nationally normed standardized achievement tests was at best hard to imagine and, to many people, a preposterous notion. But even if the idea of applying "equivalency" to homeschools formed the basis for early court decisions, laws, and regulations, there is no indication that it actually works to deliver good educational outcomes.

Laws in New Jersey, New York, Connecticut, Massachusetts, Indiana, and Kansas use the word "equivalent" in their educational statutes with respect to homeschooling. Similarly, Maryland, Delaware, and Rhode Island require that instruction be "regular and thorough." In Idaho instruction must be "comparable."[17]

In New Jersey, families are not required to initiate contact with or provide any information to authorities unless there is "credible evidence that the parent, guardian . . . is not causing the child to receive equivalent instruction." A school board may request the parents/guardians to provide proof that the child is receiving "equivalent instruction." In practice, this is rarely done.[18]

In Connecticut, the department of education promulgated voluntary guidelines that some parents follow, which act as a "safe harbor" provision, meaning that parents who follow these guidelines are deemed to be providing "equivalent instruction." The Connecticut guidelines include notifying the local superintendent that homeschooling will occur, listing the subjects to be taught, days of instruction, and the method of assessment. The guidelines provide for an annual portfolio review to assess whether instruction has been provided.[19]

In Indiana, where homeschools are considered private schools, they have been exempted from the standard of "equivalence" by statute.[20]

In Kansas families register with the state board of education, and although the law allows for enforcement proceedings to ensure that competent teachers are teaching children for an equivalent amount of time, as a practical matter, there are virtually no enforcement proceedings.[21]

All of these states have approached measuring equivalence differently—in other words, there is no equivalent way to measure equivalence. However, two states have made significant enforcement attempts to require equivalence in homeschooling that bear closer scrutiny—these are Massachusetts and New York.

The Home School Legal Defense Association (HSLDA) is the largest legal advocacy and services organization for homeschooling families. With over eighty thousand member families we receive tens of thousands of requests each year to help families when there are conflicts with school districts.

Although the National Home Education Research Institute's Dr. Brian Ray's research shows that there is no significant correlation between educational attainment of homeschooled students and the level of regulation in the state, we at HSLDA have found that there is a very high correlation of conflict between families and school authorities based on the amount of regulation.[22] New York and Massachusetts have among the most burdensome homeschool laws and also have the highest rates of conflict between schools and families.

In *Care and Protection of Charles*, its landmark ruling on home education, the Massachusetts Supreme Judicial Court (SJC) held that school committees were the appropriate body designated to "approve" home education as long as the committee was satisfied that the instruction was "equivalent in thoroughness efficiency and progress made therein" in comparison to the local schools.

The court gave guidelines to the committees allowing them ask about teacher competency (but they couldn't require degrees or training), the curriculum (subjects, hours, and materials to be used), and to require some form of periodic assessment. The SJC quoted the landmark U.S. Supreme Court cases *Pierce v. Society of Sisters* and *Wisconsin v. Yoder*, observing that parents' right to homeschool are constitutionally relevant. However, the SJC observed that such rights may be subject to balancing against the state's "substantial interest" in the education of its citizens.

The SJC established that in order to be approved as required by the state's compulsory attendance statute, a homeschooling parent was required to demonstrate that the child's education was "equal in thoroughness, efficiency and progress made therein" when compared with local schools.[23] However, a homeschooling parent who proceeded without approval would be culpable only after the school met the burden to prove that the education failed to provide this equivalent.

The result of this case has been three hundred school districts in Massachusetts with somewhat different policies and procedures and a widely varying level of enforcement of equivalence. In a subsequent ruling, *Brunelle v. Lynne Public Schools*, the SJC held that home visits were an unconstitutional condition for approving home education. In *Brunelle* the court found that

education in a home setting "can never be the equivalent of in-school education." The court also warned school committees not to apply "institutional
standards to a non-institutional setting."

The fact that each individual town has its own school committee responsible for overseeing education has resulted in idiosyncratic enforcement,
which at times has led to significant friction. For example, since 2018, a
highly contentious environment has persisted in Worcester, Massachusetts,
as the homeschooling community has objected to the imposition of what they
suggest are arbitrary and unclear standards after years of fairly low levels of
enforcement after new school personnel were assigned oversight responsibilities for homeschooling.

In its effort to enforce legislatively mandated "substantially equivalent
instruction," the New York State Board of Education issued guidelines for
homeschooling parents in 1988. Although eschewing "approval," they impose frequent and detailed interactions between individual families and
school district personnel. These interactions result in hundreds of situations
every year where HSLDA intervenes to assist homeschooling families in
resolving disputes.

The regulations require homeschooling parents to submit an initial home
instruction plan (IHIP) that includes a list of the syllabi, curriculum materials, textbooks, or a plan of instruction, and dates for the submission of quarterly reports. The quarterly reports must include

1. the number of hours of instruction during each quarter;
2. a description of the material covered in each subject;
3. a grade or narrative evaluation in each subject (the superintendent has
   no authority to judge the adequacy of these reports); and
4. a written explanation if less than 80 percent of the amount of the
   course materials as set forth in the IHIP has been covered in any
   subject.

A final assessment is also required with the last quarterly report. New York
requires standardized tests for homeschooled students every other year between fourth and eighth grade and every year for grades nine through twelve.

In recent years both New York and Massachusetts have seen litigation
relating to paperwork problems. HSLDA initiated a civil rights action when
New York City education officials failed to properly maintain reporting
paperwork, which resulted in allegations of educational neglect being made
against otherwise compliant families.

Because the children were not being taken off the attendance rolls quickly
enough, truancy allegations were referred to the social services agency that
was then dispatched to investigate—even though the families had fully com-

plied with the law. HSLDA won the lawsuit and the court ordered the city's department of education to take steps to properly follow the law.

Similarly, in Worcester, Massachusetts, a school policy required referral to children's services when a certain level of absences was recorded. A homeschooling mother's child was removed from the home for a period of seven days when her paperwork was not properly attended to, resulting in a social services investigation. HSLDA filed a civil rights action, which is pending, alleging that under Massachusetts law, school authorities have exclusive jurisdiction over school attendance and that removing a child over such concerns is a violation of her federally protected constitutional rights.

Although Massachusetts and New York (among others) retain the equivalency standards, other states realized the difficulty of enforcing and overseeing such a standard. In the 1980s, both Missouri and Minnesota Supreme Courts ruled that a statutory standard of equivalence was unconstitutionally vague when applied to homeschools. In these states today, there is virtually no conflict between school authorities and homeschooling parents regarding regulatory compliance.

Following these cases, the legislatures of both states passed statutes that spelled out specific requirements for homeschools to be in compliance with the compulsory school law. In both states, these requirements are considered to be low-level oversight. The requirements in both states related to the need to notify school authorities and provide certain demographic information. In Minnesota homeschool families were also required to assess children annually with a standardized test (although the test results are not reported to the authorities) and to submit immunization information.[24]

CONCLUSION—AN IMPERMISSIBLE STANDARD

Even if equivalence were attainable, it is a standard that the state should not impose. In a free and democratic society based on the consent of the governed, private civil society must be protected from state interference unless there is demonstrable evidence of actual harm. In *Parham* v. *J.R.*, the U.S. Supreme Court recognized that "fit parents are presumed to act in the best interests of their children."[25] This must be the standard by which we operate in all areas and especially education.

As important as education is to society, it is crucial that such a powerful societal shaping institution not be unduly controlled by the state. The consequences of such control are readily available throughout recorded history.

In *West Virginia v. Barnette* the court touched on the very heart of the matter of compulsion when it ruled that the West Virginia law requiring the Pledge of Allegiance to be recited in public schools each day on pain of expulsion and truancy prosecution was unconstitutional: "If there is any fixed star in our constitutional constellation, it is that no official, high or petty, can prescribe what shall be orthodox in politics, nationalism, religion, or other matters of opinion, or force citizens to confess by word or act their faith therein. If there are any circumstances which permit an exception, they do not now occur to us."[26]

This should be true not only in schools and in relation to pledges of allegiance, but to all aspects of a child's education. Children are born into families that should be regarded as independent social institutions that exercise protected authority with respect to the state regarding the education and upbringing of children. As a moral proposition, children in their minority require care and protection, and those who can be trusted with their welfare should be trusted to make decisions for them. This principle applies in making the decision to homeschool.

Attempting to impose equivalence as a standard to ensure children are educated to state expectations, such as in New York or Massachusetts, creates conflict and has been shown to have little to do with the quality of educational outcomes.

States that attempt to require equivalence in educational attainment or to restrict homeschooling on ideological grounds will face opposition from well-organized advocates and large numbers of parents who have demonstrated over the years a willingness and effectiveness in engaging with policy makers to protect what they consider a sacred or fundamental right.

The Massachusetts SJC was right that homeschooling cannot be measured by institutional standards of equivalence—it should not be. Sufficient evidence exists to indicate that homeschooling is effective in all relevant areas and need not be regulated at all. States have sufficient tools to intervene when credible allegations of harm are made, and the standard of equivalence contributes nothing to such concerns.

Rather than seeking to impose equivalence or more regulation on homeschooling, states should continue the trend of deregulation, which acknowledges that parents, not the government, have the prior right to decide educational matters for their children.

NOTES

1. William L. Shirer, *The Rise and Fall of the Third Reich* (New York: Simon & Schuster, 1960), 343.

2. Brian D. Ray, "Homeschooling Growing: Multiple Data Points Show Increase 2012 to 2016 and Later," National Home Education Research Institute, April 20, 2018, https://www.nheri.org/homeschool-population-size-growing/.

3. There are no authoritative records of homeschool population in other countries. I have extensive contact with other homeschooling communities and have compiled an informal estimate that supports this assertion.

4. Amber Noel, Patrick Stark, and Jeremy Redford, "Parent and Family Involvement in Education, from the National Household Education Surveys Program of 2012," NCES 2013-

028.REV2 (Washington, DC: National Center for Education Statistics, Institute of Education Sciences, U.S. Department of Education, June 2016), https://nces.ed.gov/pubs2013/2013028rev.pdf.

5. Jeremy Redford, Danielle Battle, and Stacey Bielick, "Homeschooling in the United States: 2012," NCES 2016-096.REV (Washington, DC: National Center for Education Statistics, Institute of Education Sciences, U.S. Department of Education, 2017), https://nces.edu.gov/pubs2016/2016096rev.pdf; Stacey Bielick, "1.5 Million Homeschooled Students in the United States in 2007," NCES 2009-030 (Washington, DC: National Center for Education Statistics, Institute of Education Sciences, U.S. Department of Education, December 2008), https://nces.ed.gov/pubs2009/2009030.pdf.

6. Joseph Murphy, *Homeschooling in America: Capturing and Assessing the Movement* (Thousand Oaks: Corwin Press, 2012).

7. Ibid.

8. Ibid.

9. Larry Sand, "Safe at Home," California Policy Center, August 18, 2015, https://californiapolicycenter.org/safe-at-home-teachers-union-targets-homeschooling/.

10. Thomas Spiegler, "Why State Sanctions Fail to Deter Home Education: An Analysis of Home Education in Germany and Its Implications for Home Education Policies," *Theory and Research in Education* 7, no. 3 (2009): 297–309.

11. Lawrence Burman, "Oral Decision of Immigration Judge," United States Immigration Court, Memphis, Tennessee, March 23, 2010, https://hslda.org/content/hs/international/Germany/Romeike_Official_Decision_Transcript_1-26-10.pdf.

12. Jewish Telegraphic Agency, "Chabad Leader Accuses Sweden of 'Persecuting' Couple Who Home-School Their Kids," *The Times of Israel*, October 20, 2018, https://www.timesofisrael.com/chabad-leader-accuses-sweden-of-persecuting-couple-who-home-school-their-kids/.

13. Wunderlich v. Germany, European Court of Human Rights, application no. 18925/15, January 10, 2019.

14. These are cases the author has firsthand knowledge about. See www.hslda.org for more information about these cases.

15. Michael P. Donnelly, "The Human Right of Home Education," *Journal of School Choice* 10, no. 3 (2016); Michael P. Donnelly, "State Power Versus Parental Rights: An International Human Rights Perspective on Home Education," in *Homeschooling in New View*, eds. Bruce S. Cooper, Frances R. Spielhagen, and Carlo Ricci (Charlotte: Information Age Publishing, 2016), 45–64.

16. Albert Cheng, "Does Homeschooling or Private Schooling Promote Political Intolerance? Evidence from a Christian University," *Journal of School Choice* 8, no. 1 (2014): 49–68.

17. N.J. Stat. Ann. § 18A:38-25; N.Y. Educ. Law § 3204(1); N.Y. Comp. Codes R. & Regs. tit. 8, § 100.10; Connecticut General Statutes § 10-184; Mass. Gen. Laws Ch. 76, § 1; Care and Protection of Charles, 399 Mass. 324, 504 N.E.2d 592, (1987); Ind. Code § 20-33-2-28, § Kan. Stat. Ann. 72-1111(a)(2), Md. Code Ann., Educ. § 7-301(a), 14 Del. C. § 2703A(3); R.I. Gen. Laws § 16-19-2; R.I. Gen. Laws § 16-2-2; Idaho Code § 33-202 .

18. Elizabeth Richardson, "Homeschooling Laws (or Lack Thereof) in New Jersey—Are Children Slipping Through the Cracks?," in *Journal of Law and Education* 42, no. 1 (Winter 2013): 173–81.

19. Connecticut State Department of Education, "Homeschooling in Connecticut," 2019, https://portal.ct.gov/SDE/Homeschooling/Homeschooling-in-Connecticut.

20. Ind. Code § 20-33-2-20.

21. Home School Legal Defense Association, "Homeschooling Under Your State Law: Kansas," last updated July 5, 2019, https://hslda.org/content/hs101/KS.aspx.

22. Brian D. Ray, "Home Schooling: The Ameliorator of Negative Influences on Learning?," *Peabody Journal of Education* 75, no. 1 (2000): 71–106.

23. Only Massachusetts and Rhode Island require approval for homeschooling.

24. Minn. Stat. Ann. § 120A.22; Minn. Stat. § 120A.24

25. Parham v. J. R., 442 U.S. 584 (1979).

26. West Virginia State Board of Education v. Barnette, 319 U.S. 624 (1943).

Part Four

Charting a Path Forward

Chapter Eleven

Conclusion

Rabbi Nehorai Gets the Last Word

Ira Stoll

How much power should the government of New York City and State exert over what is taught in Jewish private schools?

In addressing that question and adjacent questions, the contributors to this volume have consulted and cited a vast and diverse array of sources. To select just some highlights and examples:

Philosopher Kevin Vallier relies on reason and conceives of "the traditional liberal who embraces a presumption against state coercion." Historian Ashley Berner brings in the work of contemporary political theorists and academics, including Amy Gutmann, Meira Levinson, and William Galston, as well as the law professor Michael McConnell. Political theorist Rita Koganzon mentions the philosophers John Rawls and Eamonn Callan, the law professor Nomi Stolzenberg, and earlier thinkers such as John Locke and Jean-Jacques Rousseau.

Law professor Aaron Saiger, attorney Howard Slugh, and writer Devorah Goldman rely on opinions of the U.S. Supreme Court and of state courts, and on articles published in law journals. Charles Glenn cites accounts from the European press of increasingly frequent clashes there between religious schools and government authorities.

Lawyer Avi Schick cites the Hebrew Bible and also the historical record from newspaper accounts of an earlier clash between New York State and Jewish schools. Jay Ferguson, the head of Grace Community School in Tyler, Texas, adds the Christian Bible and the twentieth-century Christian writer C. S. Lewis. Jibran Khan, writing about Muslim schools, quotes Franz Rosenthal, a twentieth-century scholar of Islam and Arabic who was based at Yale. Lawyer and homeschool advocate Michael P. Donnelly cites the Uni-

versal Declaration of Human Rights proclaimed in 1948 by the United Nations General Assembly.

These sources and approaches all bring useful wisdom and perspective
and context. Their insights can help to guide policy makers and to enrich
public understanding of the issues and of the values and trade-offs that are
involved.

To my mind, though, the most profound and brilliant source of them all in
thinking about Jewish education in New York, what the schools should
teach, and the role of government is not Amy Gutmann, Michael McConnell,
Meira Levinson, John Rawls, C. S. Lewis, or Jean-Jacques Rousseau. It is,
rather, precisely the text that many of the students in these Jewish schools
devote the most time to studying. That is the Babylonian Talmud, whose two
main parts, the Mishna and the Gemara, were edited and compiled between
roughly 200 and 800 C.E. in the lands that are now Israel and Iraq.

This "Oral Law"—so called even though it is now written down—is held
by some traditional Jews to have been given to the Children of Israel along
with the Torah at Mount Sinai. It is a long book—2,711 two-sided pages,
divided into 63 tractates, typically printed with commentaries from sages
spanning centuries and continents surrounding the main body of the text. If
one studies a two-sided folio page a day, as many traditional Jews do, it takes
about seven and a half years to work one's way through. A complete set of
the texts, with commentaries and perhaps translations, can cost thousands of
dollars and weigh as much as an encyclopedia.

The piece of Talmud that came to mind in connection with the New York
yeshiva regulation controversy is Kiddushin 29a (the two-sided pages of the
Talmud are lettered a and b; Kiddushin is a tractate that deals with sanctify-
ing marriage, though, like nearly all the tractates, it digresses frequently to
other topics). As translated from the Mishnaic Hebrew and Aramaic in the
William Davidson digital edition of the Koren Noé Talmud, with commen-
tary by Rabbi Adin Even-Israel Steinsaltz (in nonbolded text), it says in part:

> The Gemara comments: According to this interpretation, **we learn** in this
> mishna **that which the Sages taught** in a *baraita*[1]: **A father is obligated with
> regard to his son to circumcise him, and to redeem him** if he is a firstborn
> son who must be redeemed by payment to a priest, **and to teach him Torah,
> and to marry him to a woman, and to teach him a trade. And some say:** A
> father is **also** obligated **to teach** his son **to swim. Rabbi Yehuda says: Any**
> father **who does not teach his son a trade teaches him banditry [*listut*].** The
> Gemara expresses surprise at this statement: Can it **enter your mind** that he
> actually teaches him **banditry? Rather,** the *baraita* means that it is **as though
> he teaches him banditry.** Since the son has no profession with which to
> support himself, he is likely to turn to theft for a livelihood. This *baraita*
> accords with Rav Yehuda's interpretation of the mishna.[2]

This happens actually to be a pretty widely known section of the Talmud, as these things go. The head of Jewish studies at a pluralistic Jewish day school in Brooklyn, New York, taught it to me and a group of other parents a few years ago during a study session at a synagogue to mark the Jewish holiday of Shavuot. The part about teaching to swim also appears in two-foot-high letters painted on a wall above the indoor pool at the Jewish Community Center in Newton, Massachusetts.

In these few sentences, more than 1,200 years old, are answers to many of the questions being battled over in today's yeshiva controversy. Whose obligation is the child's education? The Talmud, here at least, describes the obligation not as the community's, but as the parent's. The obligation includes teaching the child *both* a trade needed to generate income *and* the Torah. The language about learning an income-generating trade is so emphatic that it is made clear, at least in Rabbi Yehuda's opinion, that failure on that front leads inexorably, if perhaps metaphorically, to violating one of the Ten Commandments, the one against stealing.

A careful reader might find too, in the language about swimming, a nod toward a kind of pluralism: "some say." There is a respect for life, as the teaching to swim may help to protect a child from the risk of death by drowning in a region prone to dangerous flash floods. An imaginative or creative reader, or perhaps even a particularly discerning one, might discover in the language about marriage, swimming, and a trade the hope that a child will eventually, in the language of psychology, individuate, and find his own path or pool lane.

All of this comes cloaked in the authority that comes with age and revelation. With full respect to Amy Gutmann, to Meira Levinson, and even to the justices of the U.S. Supreme Court, eminent as they all surely are, their words are unlikely to be studied and remembered, much less inscribed on the walls of suburban indoor swimming pools, 1,200 years from now. There are not millions of people who devoutly believe that Gutmann's or Levinson's words were delivered at Mount Sinai.[3]

If the Talmud itself recognizes the importance of both Torah study and practical vocational education, what, then, to make of the complaints that some of New York's Jewish schools are falling short in terms of preparing students with the skills necessary for self-sufficiency? It certainly would not be the first time that some fraction of the Jewish people fell short of fully achieving an ideal set forth by the sages.

Another similarly exquisite Talmudic passage may help to explain. It comes from the end of the tractate Kiddushin, page 82b. Talmudic tractates often, but not invariably, conclude with particularly insightful or lively passages that are a way of sending students off into a traditional celebratory meal for having finished a book. In its closing sentences, Kiddushin returns to the previously raised question of the proper curriculum. Again from the Koren Noé translation, it says:

> The mishna taught that **Rabbi Nehorai says: I set aside all the trades** and I teach my son only Torah. It **is taught** in the *Tosefta*[4] (5:14): **Rabbi Nehorai says: I set aside all the trades in the world, and I teach my son only Torah, as all other trades serve one only in the days of his youth,** when he has enough strength to work, **but in the days of his old age, behold, he** is left to **lie in hunger. But Torah is not like this: It serves a person in the time of his youth and provides him with a future and hope in the time of his old age. With regard to the time of his youth, what does it say** about a Torah scholar? **"But they that wait for the Lord shall renew their strength"** (Isaiah 40:31).
>
> **With regard to** the time of **his old age, what does it say? "They shall still bring forth fruit in old age, they shall be full of sap and richness"** (Psalms 92:15).[5]

Those unfamiliar with the Talmud may find this juxtaposition confusing or contradictory. If "the sages" insist that a father is obligated to teach his son both Torah *and* a trade, why does the tractate conclude with the story of Rabbi Nehorai, who teaches "only Torah"? In the Talmud, as in Supreme Court decisions, dissenting or minority views are included for the edification of future generations and to help illuminate the underlying issues. In some cases multiple opinions are offered as a kind of recognition that multiple truths can coexist—not in a relativist way, but in a way that embraces pluralism with limits.

Even for those who understand that, though, it is difficult to escape seeing a tension between the closing anecdote in Kiddushin 82b and the earlier passage in Kiddushin 29a. Nehorai is portrayed not as a neglectful father who is effectively or deliberately cultivating a bandit, but rather as someone with a genuinely caring long-term view of his child's best interests. The sages are not recorded as having endorsed Rabbi Nehorai's approach. But the sages are not recorded, either, as having tried to interfere with Rabbi Nehorai. Nor is there any record of the sages punishing or rebuking Rabbi Nehorai for teaching his own son this way.

These two Talmudic passages—the normative language from the sages about a father's obligation, and the descriptive language about Rabbi Nehorai's dissenting practice—can be helpful in several ways in thinking about the present controversy.

They remind us, first of all, that to the extent the current conflict stems from a disagreement internal to the Jewish community, it is a long-standing disagreement, one that reaches back to when Rabbi Nehorai lived, approximately 200 C.E. Jews have been disagreeing with each other about this, in other words, for more than 1,800 years. The dominant view, then and now, emphasizes education in both Torah and a trade. But there was a dissenting view, then and now, that pursued Torah to the exclusion of a trade.

In pushing back against the curriculum of Torah and trade that was prescribed by the sages, Rabbi Nehorai was also pushing back against the dichotomy that was set up by Rabbi Yehuda between self-sufficiency and dependence. That issue is worth digging into, because it is at the center of the complaints by the contemporary advocates that prompted the new government oversight.

A 2017 report from the advocacy group Young Advocates for Fair Education contends, "Without secular education, young men lack the requisite skills to obtain employment with a decent income to support themselves and their (often large) families. . . . This puts Hasidic families at high risk for poverty and reliance upon government assistance."[6]

The U.S. Supreme Court, in its 1972 opinion in *Wisconsin v. Yoder* defending the First Amendment religious rights of Amish families to educate their children without state government interference, elaborated on the "self-sufficiency" of the Amish. The court noted that members of that religious group "reject public welfare." The justices mentioned the lack of any evidence that the Amish "would become burdens on society because of educational shortcomings."

Rabbi Nehorai reminds us that in old age, when we get too old to work, we are all inevitably dependent. From that perspective, the binary distinction between wage earners or welfare sponges, between makers or takers, becomes far less crisp; rather, over the long course of a lifetime, all of us are dependent on others at some times. That is true even for those of us who have pursued independence.

This reframing of the self-sufficiency question, from a snapshot of a single person at a single time and place to a longitudinal view over a longer period of time, can be helpful in thinking more broadly about the questions of welfare dependence and economic self-sufficiency.

Welfare dependency in New York is certainly not confined to the Orthodox Jewish community or to graduates of Jewish religious schools. In New York City overall, 60 percent of the live births in 2017 were covered by Medicaid or Family Health Plus, which are government-subsidized, income-tested health insurance programs.[7] In April 2019, 1,550,397 New York City residents, of a total population of about 8.4 million, were receiving food stamp benefits under the federal Supplementary Nutrition Assistance Program.[8]

Simply observing that the neighborhoods where the Jewish schools are have high rates of poverty and of welfare usage is not particularly useful; non-Jewish blacks and Hispanics who live in these same Brooklyn neighborhoods and who attend *public* schools also have high rates of poverty and of welfare usage.

A 2011 demographic survey focused on poverty in the Jewish community in an eight-county area that includes New York City found 22,300 "poor" Hasidic households, to focus on one variety of Orthodox Jew. It also, however, found 33,900 poor Jewish households that were "Russian-speaking senior households."[9] Most of those Russian speakers are immigrants. They attended Soviet Communist secular schools that emphasized math, science, and Russian literature, not Torah or Talmud, the teaching of which were outlawed.

If the enforcement efforts are to be based on a suspicion that a particular Jewish school is producing many welfare dependents, then no public schools are being held to similar standards. In any event, if New York politicians or advocacy groups are suddenly newly concerned about multigenerational welfare dependency, they might consider attacking the issue directly with welfare reforms instead of indirectly by stepped-up regulation of the curriculum in religious schools attended by only a small fraction of future welfare recipients.

New York's Orthodox Jewish community as a whole is not known to be more welfare dependent or poor than any other religious group; in general, it has prospered.

Two concerns other than the income, poverty, and welfare complaint are raised by proponents of additional regulation.

One has to do with the ability of yeshiva graduates to function as citizens in a democracy—as jurors, as voters. The New York State legislature in 2018 amended the 1894 law that had required private schools to offer an education "substantially equivalent" to public schools. The 2018 amendment said that in evaluating substantial equivalence, the state should consider whether a curriculum prepares students to demonstrate "an understanding of civics and the responsibilities of citizens in world communities." (Though studies have consistently found public schools to do a poor job of teaching civics.)[10]

In the *Wisconsin v. Yoder* case, as the Supreme Court's opinion described it, the state had also claimed that its involvement was required "to enable the Amish to participate effectively and intelligently in our democratic process." In the case of the Jewish schools in New York, any claim that they are producing graduates unfit to participate in politics collides with the reality that these graduates do participate actively and with some effect.

Proponents of additional regulation attempt to argue simultaneously, and with a straight face, that the Jewish schools produce illiterate, ignorant graduates and also that these same supposedly ignorant and illiterate graduates have immense political clout in New York. A 2018 *New York Times* editorial, for example, accused the yeshivas of producing graduates "bereft of even basic knowledge" and unable to sign their own names in English, while also describing the Orthodox Jewish groups as "powerful" in influencing city policy.[11]

Somehow, while lacking "basic knowledge," these yeshiva graduates also managed to generate hundreds of thousands of written comments—many of them using online forms—advocating against stricter state regulations. [12]

A third complaint of the critics of the yeshivas is that by sending children to these schools, parents are constraining not only the earning potential and political power but more broadly the possible life choices of their offspring. Even a child whose education consists solely of Torah and Talmud study, however, will find in the Talmud the language about a parent's obligation to teach his child a trade, as well as stories of children who rebel against their parents and the tradition.

The anxiety among Orthodox parents about children who go "off the way," along with the existence of a substantial nonprofit organization that exists to serve those leaving strict Orthodoxy, suggest that the fervently Orthodox are not immune from the humility that predictably awaits parents of all kinds who try to keep children on leashes that are too short.

If such cases are difficult for the person leaving the group and rare over-all, they are no less difficult or rare than when a person from a secular background attempts to become a fervently Orthodox Jew. Parents of all backgrounds attempt to guide the life choices of their children in all sorts of ways, and the success of such efforts is never guaranteed.

Defenders of the yeshivas often fall into the temptation to defend the value of Jewish education on secular grounds. Yeshivas have produced Harvard Law School students and Columbia Law School professors and at least one Nobel laureate and lots of successful Amazon.com sellers.

This may be useful as a legal or public relations strategy, but as a moral or philosophical defense, it falls short. It risks instrumentalizing the Jewish education, treating the Torah study as merely another variety of vocational education. Rabbi Nehorai avoids that error, focusing not on Torah study's utility to society overall but rather its effect in providing purpose and meaning and joy throughout the lifetime of the individual who engages in it—"future and hope in old age."

This is a values statement that may illuminate issues that go far beyond the clash between yeshivas and New York State. Non-Jewish students, too, have choices about what to study. Policy makers can influence those choices with both rhetoric and decisions about spending and regulation.

During the 2016 presidential campaign, Senator Marco Rubio, Republican of Florida, complained that the United States was producing too many philosophers and not enough welders: "We know welders make more than philosophers, but we graduate a bunch of philosophers." The Democratic presidential candidate in 2016, Hillary Clinton, picked up that theme, too. [13]

In 2014, President Barack Obama apologized to a University of Texas art historian after saying in a speech, "folks can make a lot more, potentially, with skilled manufacturing or the trades than they might with an art history degree." In his apology, Obama wrote, "As it so happens, art history was one of my favorite subjects in high school, and it has helped me take in a great deal of joy in my life that I might otherwise have missed." [14]

College students are increasingly choosing to major in "practical" fields such as computer science and engineering rather than in English or history. That has lots of causes, including the left-wing politicization of the humanities and the needs of graduates to earn income to repay the soaring cost of college, but as students and policy makers navigate the decisions about what to study and why, they can look to both Rabbi Nehorai and Rabbi Yehuda as guides in thinking through what is important.

Even if secular society chooses not to learn from the Talmud, at least the book's wisdom will be there for those in the Jewish community who value it. The Talmud has endured despite attempts by enemies over the years at banning it, burning it, or, as New York seems at risk of doing, trying essentially to outlaw the intensive study of it.

The philosopher Emmanuel Levinas (1906–1995) wrote, "The famous 'study of the Torah' is, for Jewish piety, the fulfilment of a divine will, as worthy as obedience to all the other commandments combined. It has preserved Israel throughout the ages. . . . The oral Torah . . . extracts ethical meaning as the ultimate intelligibility of the human and even of the cosmic." [15]

As a guide to public policy, "divine will" can have its drawbacks, or at least limits. When people disagree about what the divine will is, as they often do, God can be reticent about weighing in directly, leaving his position at times frustratingly obscure. Even for believers, it can seem as if there is a lot left to fill in. Readers of the Talmud never find out, for example, what became of Rabbi Nehorai's son.

How did Rabbi Nehorai's son earn a living? Was his old age indeed full of richness? Did he lead an ethical life? Did he have children? And if so, how did he educate them—according to his father's example, with only Torah, or according to the instruction of the other sages, with Torah and a trade and some say even teaching to swim?

We do not hear from Rabbi Nehorai many other times in the Talmud. One of the other instances comes in Avot 4:14: "Rabbi Nehorai said: Exile yourself to a place of Torah, and do not assume that it will come after you, for your fellow students will ensure that it will remain with you. Do not rely on your own understanding." [16] The author and teacher Rabbi Jonathan Sacks comments: "Be prepared to travel to a centre of Torah study where there are outstanding teachers and scholars. Torah is learned not only from books but also, and essentially, from people, their conduct, and the fellowship of argument." [17]

If New York renders itself inhospitable to the rigorous and intensive study of Jewish texts, Rabbi Nehorai seems to be advising from the past, scholars should not hesitate to leave for other places.

In the long sweep of Jewish history, after all, the Jewish presence in New York, even at more than 350 years old, is relatively brief. Many of the yeshivas came to New York only in the twentieth century after the destruction of Eastern European Jewry under Communism and Nazism. If necessary, these schools, teachers, and students could be moved.

Lakewood, New Jersey, which is near New York and where there are already tens of thousands of Orthodox Jewish students, might be one possible destination. So is Israel, though with clear eyes about the reality that even the Israeli public has limits on its willingness to pay for yeshiva students who do not otherwise engage in paid work. Travel is now easier than it has been for most of Jewish history, and the Jewish state provides a refuge.

As long as the United States and New York have existed, they have protected religious liberty and the Jews. An honest reading of Jewish history, though, suggests that, outside of Israel, even the most hospitable such refuges are temporary in nature. One hopes it does not come to that. If it does, though, the descendants of Rabbi Yehuda and of Rabbi Nehorai may yet find that the words of the Torah are not only a more valuable philosophical source than are the words of the U.S. Constitution or New York State law, but also that they provide better practical advice and protection.

NOTES

1. A *baraita* is a text from the time of the Mishnah (approximately 200 C.E.) that was not included in the Mishnah.
2. Kiddushin 29a (The William Davidson Talmud), https://www.sefaria.org/.
3. To be fair, the feeling that certain Democratic constituency groups have for selected Supreme Court decisions—*Roe v. Wade*, if not *Bush v. Gore*—does approach and may even at times surpass religious fervor.
4. The *Tosefta* is a compilation of texts from the period of the Mishnah (approximately 200 C.E.) that were not included in the Mishnah.
5. Kiddushin 82b.
6. Alisa Partlan et al., "Non-Equivalent: The State of Education in New York City's Hasidic Yeshivas," Young Advocates for Fair Education (Yaffed, Inc.) (2017), https://www.yaffed.org/report.
7. New York State Department of Health, "Live Births by Primary Financial Coverage and Resident County, New York State 2017," July 2019, https://www.health.ny.gov/statistics/vital_statistics/2017/table13.htm.
8. City of New York, "Total SNAP Recipients," NYC OpenData, June 17, 2019, https://data.cityofnewyork.us/Social-Services/Total-SNAP-Recipients/5c4s-jwtq.
9. Jacob B. Ukeles, Steven M. Cohen, and Ron Miller, "Jewish Community Study of New York: 2011: Special Report on Poverty." UJA-Federation of New York, June 2013, 54, https://www.ujafedny.org/assets/785329.
10. "Annenberg Civics Knowledge Survey," Annenberg Public Policy Center, University of Pennsylvania, 2019, https://www.annenbergpublicpolicycenter.org/political-communication/civics-knowledge-survey/; "NAEP Civics," National Center for Education Statistics, Institute of Education Sciences, U.S. Department of Education, November 15, 2018, https://nces.ed.gov/nationsreportcard/civics/.
11. The Editorial Board of the *New York Times*, "New York's Yeshiva Students Deserve Better: Elected Officials Should Require Orthodox Jewish Schools to Meet Legal Standards,"

New York Times, August 23, 2018, https://www.nytimes.com/2018/08/23/opinion/yeshiva-orthodox-jews-deblasio.html.

12. The Yeshiva World, "Staggering Numbers: More Than 135,000 Comments Opposing Proposed Regulation to Yeshiva Education Sent to State," *The Yeshiva World*, September 4, 2019, https://www.theyeshivaworld.com/news/general/1783852/staggering-numbers-more-than-135000-comments-opposing-proposed-regulation-to-yeshiva-education-sent-to-state.html.

13. Ira Stoll, "Clinton Campaign Themes Failed to Resonate for Jeb Bush and Rubio," *New York Sun*, April 25, 2016, https://www.nysun.com/national/clinton-campaign-themes-failed-to-resonate/89556/.

14. Aamer Madhani, "Obama Apologizes for Joking about Art History Majors," *USA Today*, February 19, 2014, https://www.usatoday.com/story/theoval/2014/02/19/obama-apologizes-to-texas-art-history-professor/5609089/.

15. Emmanuel Levinas, *Nine Talmudic Readings*, trans. Annette Aronowicz (Bloomington: Indiana University Press, 1990), 91–93.

16. Pirkei Avot 4.

17. *The Authorised Daily Prayer Book of the United Hebrew Congregations of the Commonwealth*, trans. Simeon Singer and Jonathan Sacks (London: Collins, 2007), 551.

Index

Abraham, 93
accountability: in common-school position, 19; in individual rights, 21; in liberal pluralism, 24, 25
Adh-Dhahabī, 111
Administrative Procedure Act (APA), xviii
Agudath Israel girls' school, 82
Alito, Samuel, 74
America: curriculum variety in, 18; diversity of, 108; Islamic education in, 113–114, 114, 117–118; Jewish population in, xi; Jews' education struggle in, xiv–xv; Orthodox Jewish population in, xi; teachers' political leanings in, 43n15
American homeschooling, 127, 132; *Care and Protection of Charles* in, 129; in Connecticut, 128; HSLDA in, 129, 130–131; in Indiana, 128; in Kansas, 128; in Massachusetts, 129–130, 131, 132; in Minnesota, 131; in New Jersey, 128; in NYS, 129, 130–131; *Parham* v. *J.R.* in, 131; Pledge of Allegiance and, 131–132; *West Virginia v. Barnette* in, 131–132
Amish, 31; independence of, 33, 34. *See also Wisconsin v. Yoder*
Amish compared to Hasidic Jews, 33–34, 34–35, 44n16. *See also* First Amendment
Antin, Mary, 77

APA. *See* Administrative Procedure Act
Arabic language, 112, 115, 116, 120n6, 120n13; as Divine Speech, 112; rhetoric in, 112
Aramaic language, 13n5, 39, 138
Austria, 76, 79
Austrian *Federal Constitution*, 76
autonomy: individual rights and, 22; in Rawlsian argument, 34, 43n15; state control and, 18. *See also* yeshiva autonomy defense

Babylonians, xiii
Babylonian Talmud, 138–139
Barack Fishman, Sylvia, 96
baraita, 138, 145n1
Beis Yaakov High School for Girls, 80–81
Belgium: Europe's government supervision resistance in, 79–80, 82; Jewish day schools in, 78
Bellah, Robert, 102
Bender, Yaakov, 97
Berner, Ashley, 119
Bible reading, 102–103
bilingualism, 22–23
Brazil homeschooling, 127
Britain, 77–78, 78, 85; values regulation in, 97–98
Brown v. Board of Education (1954), 23
Brunelle v. Lynne Public Schools, 129–130
bureaucracy, 18, 27n18

About the Contributors

Jason Bedrick is director of policy for EdChoice and an adjunct scholar with the Cato Institute. He previously served as a legislator in the New Hampshire House of Representatives and was an education policy research fellow at the Josiah Bartlett Center for Public Policy.

Ashley Berner is deputy director of the Johns Hopkins Institute for Education Policy, associate professor of education, and the author of *Pluralism and American Public Education: No One Way to School* (2017). She has published numerous articles, book chapters, and op-eds on citizenship formation, academic outcomes, and teacher preparation in different national contexts.

Michael Donnelly is HSLDA senior counsel and director of global outreach and teaches constitutional law as an adjunct professor at Patrick Henry College. He and his wife homeschool their seven children. His practice and research areas include international human rights, parental rights in education, religious freedom, and home education.

Jay Ferguson is the head of school of Grace Community School in Tyler, Texas. He is an adjunct professor at Covenant College, Gordon College, and Dallas Baptist University and recently served on the adjunct faculties at Calvin College and at Peabody College of Education at Vanderbilt University. Prior to working in education, he served as a litigator in Texas for ten years. Jay and his wife, Ashley, have three daughters: Emma, Annie, and Ellen.

Charles L. Glenn is professor emeritus of educational leadership and policy studies at Boston University, where he taught for twenty-five years. From

1970 to 1991 Glenn headed the office responsible for equity and urban education at the Massachusetts Department of Education. He has published more than a dozen books on historical and comparative educational policy and has advised in a number of states and countries on educational equity.

Devorah Goldman is a visiting fellow at the Ethics and Public Policy Center. Her writing has appeared in *The Weekly Standard*, *National Affairs*, *The American Interest*, *Jewish Action*, *Regulation*, *Bloomberg BNA*, and other publications.

Jay P. Greene is distinguished professor and chair of the Department of Education Reform at the University of Arkansas. Greene's work has been published in journals from a diverse set of disciplines, including education, sociology, public policy, psychology, political science, and economics. He has also written or edited three prior books, including *Failure Up Close* with Michael Q. McShane (Rowman & Littlefield, 2018).

Jibran Khan currently serves as the editor at the National Interest Foundation in Washington, D.C. He was formerly the 2017–2019 Thomas L. Rhodes Fellow at the National Review Institute. In addition to his policy and writing work, he is a student of the traditional Muslim sciences at Al-Maqasid in Pennsylvania.

Rita Koganzon is associate director of the Program on Constitutionalism and Democracy and a lecturer in the Politics Department at the University of Virginia. Her research focuses on questions of childhood, education, and the family, and her work has appeared in both scholarly and popular publications, including *National Affairs*, the *Hedgehog Review*, *The Point*, and the *Chronicle of Higher Education*.

Matthew H. Lee, a former high school history teacher, is an education policy researcher for the Department of Education Reform at the University of Arkansas, where his research interests include educational liberty and religious education. He lives in Fayetteville, Arkansas, with his wife Caroline and his son Theo.

Aaron Saiger is a professor of law at Fordham Law School, where he teaches about education and regulatory law. He clerked for Judge Douglas Ginsburg of the U.S. Court of Appeals for the District of Columbia Circuit, and for Justice Ruth Bader Ginsburg of the U.S. Supreme Court. His current scholarly projects address school choice, school governance, and educational technology. His book, *Schoolhouse in the Cloud*, is in progress.

Avi Schick is a partner at Troutman Sanders. He spent a decade as a senior New York State government official, serving as deputy attorney general, and then as president of the state's economic development agency. He has litigated important religious liberty cases, including the challenge to New York's regulations of religious and independent schools, and has written about religion and the law for the *New York Times*, *Wall Street Journal*, the *New Republic*, and *Slate*.

Howard Slugh is an attorney practicing in Washington, D.C. He is a co-founder and general counsel at the Jewish Coalition for Religious Liberty.

Ira Stoll is managing editor of *Education Next*, an education policy journal based at Harvard University's Program on Education Policy and Governance. He is the author of *Samuel Adams: A Life* and *JFK, Conservative*. He is a columnist of the *Algemeiner* and of the *New York Sun*, and he is editor of FutureOfCapitalism.com.

Kevin Vallier is an associate professor of philosophy at Bowling Green State University. His interests lie within political philosophy, political economy, normative ethics, and philosophy of religion. His books include *Liberal Politics and Public Faith: Beyond Separation* and *Must Politics Be War? Restoring Our Trust in the Open Society*.